INTERNATIONAL DEVELOPMENT IN FOCUS

Spatial Planning for Resilient Economic Diversification

La Guajira, Colombia

JAMES DOBBIN, TATIANA MÁRQUEZ, AND JENNIFER RIETBERGEN-MCCRACKEN

WORLD BANK GROUP

1818 H Street NW, Washington, DC 20433
Telephone: 202-473-1000; Internet: www.worldbank.org

1 2 3 4 24 23 22 21

ISBN: 978-1-4648-1713-7
DOI: 10.1596/978-1-4648-1713-7

Cover photo: © James Dobbin / Dobbin International. Used with the permission of James Dobbin / Dobbin International. Further permission required for reuse.

Cover design: Debra Naylor / Naylor Design Inc.

Contents

Boxes

Figures

Maps

Photos

Tables

Acknowledgments

This report was commissioned by the World Bank's Extractives-Led Local Economic Diversification (ELLED) Program, a knowledge program that supports inclusive growth in mineral- and hydrocarbon-rich countries through innovation, long-term competitiveness, and regional synergies.

The report documents the use of a strategic spatial development planning approach to identify sustainable economic diversification opportunities in mining-dependent regions. The report complements an earlier World Bank publication, *Building Resilience: A Green Growth Framework for Mobilizing Mining Investment* (Sekar et al. 2019), which investigated the potential for leveraging the mining industry to drive the uptake of climate-sensitive technologies and practices in emerging and developing markets.

The report was authored by a team comprising James Dobbin (Project Director and Spatial Planner), Tatiana Márquez (Spatial Planner and Environmental Engineer), and Jennifer Rietbergen-McCracken (Senior Sustainable Development Analyst), with contributions from Jack Ruitenbeek (Environment and Development Economist), all from Dobbin International. Preparation of the report was supervised by Silvana Tordo, ELLED Program Team Leader and Lead Energy Economist, Energy and Extractives Global Practice of the World Bank, who also provided editorial improvements together with Fayre Makeig.

Dobbin International developed a proprietary strategic spatial development planning approach and methodology to analyze geospatial data and identify strategic plans, investment projects, and costed development policy options. This methodology has been applied in the La Guajira department as well as in other mining and nonmining regions and is described in this report.

The team would like to thank the Extractives Global Programmatic Support,[1] a multidonor trust fund administered by the Energy and Extractives Global Practice, for financial support.

Special thanks go to the Cerrejón mine and Juan Carlos Garcia (Social Affairs Manager), Linoska Mendoza (Analyst), and Luz Nidia Pedreros (Coordinator) for their cooperation, as well as to peer reviewers Javier Aguilar (Senior Mining Specialist), Michael Stanley (Lead Mining Specialist), and Kristina Svensson (Country Manager, Somalia and Mining Sector Expert).

The team would also like to thank the following members of the Dobbin International team, who were involved in preparing the original La Guajira project: Julio Galindo, Beatriz Giraldo, Laura Hernández, Guoping Huang, Juan David Linares, Alba Lucia Montoya de Beltrán, María Isabel Olarte, María del Pilar Hernández, and John Taylor.

This report is largely based on the technical report *Strategy for Sustainable and Resilient Development of La Guajira, Colombia* (Dobbin International 2020).

NOTE

1. Further information about the Extractives Global Programmatic Support may be found at the fund's website, https://www.worldbank.org/en/programs/egps.

REFERENCES

Dobbin International. 2020. *Strategy for Sustainable and Resilient Development of La Guajira, Colombia*. Report prepared for Cerrejón mine, La Guajira (Spanish). Herndon, VA: Dobbin International.

Sekar, S., K. Lundin, C. Tucker, J. Figueiredo, S. Tordo, and J. Aguilar. 2019. *Building Resilience: A Green Growth Framework for Mobilizing Mining Investment*. International Development in Focus. Washington, DC: World Bank. doi:10.1596/978-1-4648-1426-6.

About the Authors

James Dobbin established Dobbin International in 1976 to undertake strategic spatial development planning of land, coast, and ocean areas. Since 1980 he has led spatial planning projects related specifically to extractives projects in the Canadian High Arctic, Colombia, Gabon, Guinea, Madagascar, Mozambique, South Africa, and the United States. Dobbin International's clients include international multilateral organizations, United Nations organizations, international nongovernmental organizations, numerous government ministries, bilateral development agencies, communities, and private sector extractive companies such as Anadarko Petroleum Corporation, Anglo American, Anglo American Platinum, Cerrejón mine, DeBeers Group of Companies, and Rio Tinto. As a pioneer in this field, James has undertaken hundreds of spatial planning projects in more than 106 countries around the world. He has published extensively, including conference papers, and made numerous presentations on the role of spatial planning to improve development outcomes. He holds a master's degree of landscape architecture in regional environmental planning and a bachelor's degree of landscape architecture in regional environmental planning.

Tatiana Márquez has worked with Dobbin International since 2015 on spatial development planning projects in Colombia, Guinea, and South Africa. As a spatial planner and project manager, Tatiana has international experience in the development of geospatial databases, spatial modeling, planning strategy formulation, and development of ecosystems and agriculture adaptation measures against climate change. In addition, Tatiana has experience in the preparation of social and environmental assessments of large- and small-scale agroindustry projects including those focused on oil palm, rubber, and sugar cane, among others. Tatiana holds a master's degree in urban and environmental planning as a Fulbright Scholar and a bachelor's degree in environmental engineering.

Jennifer Rietbergen-McCracken has worked with Dobbin International since 2012 on spatial development planning projects in Colombia, Guinea, Mozambique, and South Africa. As an independent consultant, her clients have included international organizations such as the International Finance Corporation, International Union for Conservation of Nature, United Nations Conference on Trade and Development, United Nations Environment Programme, and the World Bank as well as bilateral development agencies and international nongovernmental organizations. Jennifer served as head of research for the Responsible Mining Foundation from 2016 to 2019. Her areas of expertise include analyzing mining companies' policies and practices on economic, environmental, governance, and social issues; researching social and participatory development issues; developing and applying assessment and planning methodologies; and providing policy analysis and advice on the integration of poverty reduction and conservation. She holds a master's of science degree in environmental technology.

Report Context

"More comprehensive, multi-sector investment planning methods that are capable of exploring, identifying, and effectively mobilizing synergies within and across geographic areas (national and regional), economic sectors, and socio-economic groups have become today essential methods in the poverty reduction 'tool-box' in developing countries. While spatial development planning initiatives are more complex and expensive to undertake, they invariably yield much higher and more sustainable benefits to the local, sub-national, national and regional communities."

World Bank (2010), Mozambique Spatial Development Planning Technical Assistance Project (P121398)

WHAT DOES THIS REPORT AIM TO DO?

This report aims to illustrate how a strategic spatial development planning approach, which has often been used in mining-related contexts, aligns closely with the green growth framework and expands the framework by extending its application to a broader set of mining-informed growth sectors. The report describes how the planning approach has been used to gain new insights into the opportunities and constraints of a mining-dependent region and to develop a multisectoral development plan. Such a plan would help to

- *Diversify the local economy* to build resilience and reduce dependence on mining revenue;
- *Conserve and enhance the region's natural capital* and account for climate change implications to ensure sustainable, productive use of environmental resources; and
- *Capitalize on green-growth-based development opportunities* through private and public sector investment and partnerships in the short, medium, and long terms.

A more diversified economy would also provide a wider range of employment and investment opportunities that would facilitate a potential future transition away from coal mining. However, this report does not advocate for coal mine closure, nor does it provide a detailed analysis of the technical, environmental, and social steps associated with coal mine closure and a just transition.

WHO IS THE REPORT ADDRESSED TO?

This report will be of interest to various groups, including (1) the extractives community, particularly those interested in the concepts of creating shared value, collaborative development planning, and planning for closure and postclosure; (2) proponents and practitioners of green growth; and (3) policy makers and policy advisers interested in innovative approaches to development planning at national, regional, departmental, or local scales.

WHAT DO WE MEAN BY "GREEN GROWTH"?

Green growth is defined as "fostering economic growth and development while ensuring that natural assets continue to provide the resources and environmental services on which our well-being relies" (OECD 2011, 9). A recent World Bank report, *Building Resilience: A Green Growth Framework for Mobilizing Mining Investment*, presents a strategic approach for mining companies and policy makers to identify high-impact opportunities for green growth (Sekar et al. 2019). The report describes the focus of green growth strategies as ensuring that "natural assets can deliver their full economic potential on a sustainable basis. To achieve this objective, green growth strategies must catalyze the investment and innovation that underpin sustained growth and generate new economic opportunities."

The concepts of green growth and sustainable development are similar, although the second is broader. Green growth implies a specific focus on finding innovative ways to leverage natural resource wealth for broad-based, climate-proofed economic growth, while maintaining healthy, productive ecosystems.

WHAT IS "STRATEGIC SPATIAL DEVELOPMENT PLANNING"?

The objective of the planning approach outlined here is to identify an implementable growth strategy in a given geographical area. The resultant strategy takes advantage of synergies across multiple sectors, while respecting broad principles of sustainable development. These principles can also give weight to green growth, nature conservation, and climate-proofed natural resource management.

The spatial planning approach presented in this report was developed by Dobbin International and has often been used within the context of large-scale mining operations to develop initiatives that can be implemented by the concerned mining companies, other actors (the private sector, the government, or nongovernmental organizations), or through multistakeholder collaborative programs. The approach considers a wide range of administrative, biophysical, environmental, social, and economic factors and encompasses multiple sectors that offer direct contributions to green growth, typically including agriculture, forestry, tourism, energy, infrastructure, and urban development. Most often focused at a regional level and including planning zones down to the local level, the approach takes into account national and international contexts and opportunities.

REFERENCES

OECD (Organisation for Economic Co-operation and Development). 2011. *Towards Green Growth.* Paris: OECD Publishing. doi:10.1787/9789264111318-en.

Sekar, S., K. Lundin, C. Tucker, J. Figueiredo, S. Tordo, and J. Aguilar. 2019. *Building Resilience: A Green Growth Framework for Mobilizing Mining Investment*. International Development in Focus. Washington, DC: World Bank. doi:10.1596/978-1-4648-1426-6.

World Bank. 2010. "Project Appraisal Document on a Proposed Credit in the Amount of SDR13.6 Million (US$20 Million Equivalent) to the Republic of Mozambique for a Spatial Development Planning Technical Assistance Project." Washington, DC: World Bank. http://documents1.worldbank.org/curated/en/225861468062683337/pdf/562760PAD0P1211C0disclosed091151101.pdf.

Executive Summary

La Guajira is a region of stark contrasts and contradictions. It is home to one of the largest coal mining operations in the world yet suffers from the highest rates of poverty, child mortality, and illiteracy in the country. It has been identified as one of Colombia's most climate-vulnerable departments but also the one with the greatest potential for solar and wind energy production. It has an extensive coastline but desert-like conditions. Its economy is largely based on coal but has huge potential for other resource-based industries such as agriculture, forestry, and tourism. La Guajira also stands out as the most ethnically diverse department in the country; indigenous groups—primarily the Wayuu people—and Afro-Colombians represent nearly 60 percent of the department´s total population. The COVID-19 pandemic has highlighted the Wayuu's vulnerability to food insecurity and malnutrition, while high levels of immigration from República Bolivariana de Venezuela have exacerbated socioeconomic challenges and social instability.

The department is strikingly reliant on mining. The Cerrejón mine generates revenue equivalent to 45 percent of La Guajira's gross domestic product (GDP) and contributes nearly a quarter of Colombia's total mining revenue. At the same time, mining operations are suffering from a shrinking international market as countries phase out their use of thermal coal to support green growth and climate action. In this context, Colombia's environmental and green growth policies seek to address a complexity of issues including economic competitiveness, climate action, social inclusion, and sustainable use of the country's natural wealth.

This report illustrates how spatial planning is being used in the department of La Guajira to guide economic diversification policies and investment activity aimed at increasing the department's economic and social resilience. The report documents a planning exercise initiated by the Cerrejón mine in 2019, undertaken by Dobbin International, and includes examples of spatial planning initiatives in other countries where the same approach was applied (Guinea, Madagascar, Mozambique, and South Africa).

Consultations with a wide range of stakeholder groups complemented an extensive process of data gathering, mapping, spatial analysis, and expert interpretation. Scenario-based spatial suitability models were produced, covering the most promising economic drivers for La Guajira as well as support drivers needed to underpin green growth in the department. The resultant action plan and prioritized set of high-value investments, if implemented, will generate significant employment and economic benefits to strengthen the department's resilience and, in the event of mine closure, mitigate the worst socioeconomic impacts.

The spatial planning approach illustrated in this case study has been applied in both mining and nonmining contexts and aligns strongly with the green growth framework set out in the World Bank report *Building Resilience: A Green Growth Framework for Mobilizing Mining Investment* (Sekar et al. 2019). Central to the approach are (1) identification of scalable opportunities based on sustainable management and/or rehabilitation of the area's natural resource base for productive uses and (2) development of an integrated set of multisectoral investments that takes full advantage of potential cross-sectoral synergies. In La Guajira, this approach enabled the planning team[1] to identify ecosystems and areas that can perform joint functions. An intact mangrove ecosystem, for example, will absorb storm wind energy while also sequestering carbon, filtering municipal sewage, and providing a nursery ground for nearshore fisheries. And an urban flood-prone area has been designated a no-build "sponge park" zone: playing fields that could be quickly and temporarily converted when necessary into water storage areas to mitigate flooding. Other insights gained include the following:

- *The poorest, most water-stressed area has strong potential.* The poorest area, in the north of La Guajira, is also the area with the highest level of land degradation (driven in part by the overgrazing of sheep and goats) and least accessibility, due to the very poor conditions of the limited road network. At the same time, the planning showed that this is also the most promising area for wind and solar energy production and has strong potential for date palm plantations, mesquite, and prickly pear cactus. In addition, while the northern area is highly water stressed and rivers here flow only in the rainy season, analysis of the department hydrogeological map shows zones of high lineament density (indicating groundwater recharge areas) and absorbent soils. Hence, with appropriate water-retention interventions (such as check dams and riparian buffer zones), the area has high water availability and recharge potential.
- *Renewable energy projects are promising—but their placement, as currently planned, is suboptimal.* Spatial analyses revealed that while La Guajira offers strong potential for renewable energy, upcoming wind and solar energy projects are all planned for suboptimal locations, that is, along the northern and northeastern coasts. Installing wind turbines in these areas would compromise the attractiveness of these high-potential tourism zones, create potential conflicts with bird migration routes, and generate less energy than if they were located inland. The planning identified areas in Upper Guajira as the most suitable locations for wind and solar farms, based on their more favorable wind and solar conditions and the fact that these installations would not conflict with other land uses in this sparsely populated zone.
- *Goat production can be compatible with environmental as well as cultural values.* Goats have a strong economic and cultural importance for the Wayuu population, as symbols of wealth, as easily liquidated assets, and as sources of meat. Currently, the large number of goats and sheep in La Guajira (estimated at 1.5 million) presents considerable environmental challenges, as evidenced

by the denuded landscapes and widespread erosion seen in the northern section of the department. Spatial analyses enabled the identification of a potential solution that respects both local culture and the environment—to switch from a free-roaming to a zero-grazing, corral-based system, which would increase the profitability of goat and sheep production while protecting and enhancing the vulnerable landscapes. The analyses also indicated that this area is suitable for cultivating two native crops—mesquite (a small leguminous tree) and prickly pear cactus (a succulent)—for use as goat fodder and for revegetation, aiding soil conservation and water management.
- *The department has strong and unmet tourism potential.* La Guajira is renowned locally, nationally, and internationally for offering unique tourism experiences in remote areas, from bird watching in a 7,000-hectare flamingo reserve to kite surfing, that take advantage of the department's strong winds and beautiful beaches. The spatial analyses revealed potential to enhance the current tourism offerings and expand into specialized markets, and identified five distinct tourism corridors.
- *Cross-sectoral synergies will facilitate broad-based growth.* The analyses showed where coordinated investments in different sectors can boost development gains. For example, removing key constraints to tourism development by improving connectivity (Wi-Fi and cellular) and infrastructure (roads, ports, landing strips, and airports) would open the area for renewable energy installations and agricultural and fisheries development, as well as enhance access to health and education facilities and banking and government services.
- *Mining infrastructure can be reused to support broad-based economic diversification.* Given the planned closure of the Cerrejón mine by 2034, the analysis considered potential reuse options for the current mining infrastructure, including the airports, the railroad, the port of Puerto Bolivar, the administrative offices, mine pits, and compensation areas. Although detailed prefeasibility studies will be necessary, the analyses uncovered opportunities to support the export of local goods via the port, transport tourists using the railroad, create water reservoirs in the pits, and possibly establish a national park in the compensation area, a dry tropical forest, that would connect the Sierra Nevada de Santa Marta with the Serranía del Perijá.
- *Inclusion of Wayuu and local communities is critical for development planning.* La Guajira is a multicultural department, with most of its territory belonging to indigenous communities. Going forward, it is necessary to consult with these communities regarding any investments or initiatives. The analyses highlighted best practices for integrating Wayuu local communities' participation and insights in the development of potential opportunities for employment generation and sustainable development.

The planning in La Guajira culminated in the development of a "project bank" of 112 initiatives and 28 prioritized projects. Of the prioritized projects, 13 high-impact projects were chosen for an in-depth analysis of their economic viability and socioeconomic impact. The analysis revealed great potential for significant improvements in economic growth, employment, income generation, and poverty reduction. For example, the proposed investments in ports and roads were estimated to provide more than 8,500 jobs during the life of these projects, while the proposed agricultural initiatives were estimated to account for the bulk (75 percent) of the potential employment generation benefits, which total nearly 50,000 jobs by 2040. This increased employment was estimated to generate a 65 percent increase in per capita income in the department. On this basis, assuming the 13 priority projects are implemented (entailing a US$660 million investment) and the Cerrejón mine closes in 2034, the department's GDP was estimated to reach US$5.2 billion within the same time frame, based on 2018 prices. By comparison, the current annual GDP in La Guajira is approximately US$3.5 billion, and the department's recently approved development plan for 2020–24 envisages investing only 5.85 percent of the total budget envelope of US$460 million in economic diversification and strategic infrastructure projects.

Implementation of a fuller set of projects, totaling an investment of nearly US$2 billion, would enable the department's GDP to reach US$8.2 billion by 2040, more than offsetting the impact of mine closure in 2034. This increased investment would replace mining revenue with a diversified economy built on increased agriculture, tourism, infrastructure, forest plantations, commerce, and, possibly, fishing and mariculture.

Selected environmental benefits were also identified and their value was estimated. For example, potential land-use changes yield greenhouse gas reductions of more than 40 million tons of carbon dioxide equivalent annually. This mitigation would represent an annual value equivalent to US$2.4 billion, at carbon prices consistent with those required to achieve targets under the Paris Agreement.[2]

The spatial planning approach is not infallible. It takes more than financial resources to be successful. Certain conditions need to be in place, including stakeholders' collaboration throughout the planning phase, a strong up-front commitment to follow through on implementation of the plans, and a truly multisectoral approach underpinned by creative thinking and a holistic focus on systems. Government support for, and participation in, the planning process is essential to ensure follow-up and alignment with public sector policies and strategies. National and regional governments can play critical roles in initiating, coconvening, or mandating collaboration. As with any planning approach, the real value of a plan lies in its subsequent implementation. While implementation may be affected by many factors (including, for example, the extent to which the different stakeholders involved share the same vision and commitment), the collaborative nature of strategic spatial development planning helps create the necessary conditions for buy-in and follow-up by the different actors involved. Key mechanisms to support the coordinated implementation of plans include (1) multistakeholder committees with strong representation of local communities and (2) investment platforms.

Given the successes seen in using this planning approach in different contexts, it offers strong potential for further rollout. Whether undertaken within development assistance programs, shared value initiatives, or public sector planning, the approach can help mainstream green growth at multiple levels.

NOTES

1. The planning team comprises professionals from Dobbin International, including multidisciplinary spatial planners, economists, agriculture specialists, environmental engineers, satellite image analysts, and researchers.
2. The Paris Agreement is an international treaty on climate change adopted by 196 parties at the United Nations Framework Convention on Climate Change, held in Paris in December 2015. Its goal is to keep global warming below an upper threshold increase of 2 degrees Celsius.

REFERENCE

Sekar, S., K. Lundin, C. Tucker, J. Figueiredo, S. Tordo, and J. Aguilar. 2019. *Building Resilience: A Green Growth Framework for Mobilizing Mining Investment*. International Development in Focus. Washington, DC: World Bank. doi:10.1596/978-1-4648-1426-6.

Abbreviations

CO_2	carbon dioxide
CRD	Committee for Regional Development
DI	Dobbin International
GDP	gross domestic product
GHG	greenhouse gas
NDC	nationally determined contribution
NGO	nongovernmental organization
NTFP	nontimber forest product
RDF	Regional Development Framework
tCO_2e	tons of carbon dioxide equivalent

1 Strategic Spatial Development Planning in La Guajira: Context

OBJECTIVES AND DRIVERS

The overall objective of the strategic spatial development planning in La Guajira was to identify and evaluate opportunities and constraints for development of the area, based on reliable data, and prepare a strategic action plan to unlock the full potential of the department and its surroundings.[1] The planning initiative, undertaken by Dobbin International, identified actionable investments in green growth that promise to enhance the department's competitiveness and diversify its economic base while also contributing to the resolution of structural social problems in La Guajira. These benefits would, in turn, mitigate the socioeconomic impact of the Cerrejón mine's eventual closure (planned for 2034). It is important to bear in mind that revenue from the mine is currently equivalent to approximately 45 percent of the department's gross domestic product (GDP), so maintaining this level of revenue postclosure through green growth initiatives is an ambitious undertaking.

NATIONAL CONTEXT

The Colombian government has pursued a green growth strategy as part of its efforts to move to a low-carbon economy and reduce its dependency on mining (mainly of coal, which accounts for a significant proportion of the country's exports). Colombia's 2018 Green Growth Policy aims to stimulate an increase in productivity and economic competitiveness by 2030, while ensuring sustainable use of natural capital and social inclusion in a manner compatible with climate change (see box 1.1) (CNPD 2019).

Colombia is highly vulnerable to the impacts of climate change, particularly flooding along its extensive coastline. While its current green energy use (hydroelectricity provides 70 percent of domestic energy needs) is likewise vulnerable to climate change effects, the country has strong potential for generation of solar, wind, and biomass energy (IPS 2018).

Colombia faces a severe economic downturn due to domestic and international impacts of the COVID-19 pandemic, exacerbated by low oil and coal prices and reduced demand for coal in the medium to long term.

BOX 1.1

Colombia's Green Growth Policy and climate change commitment

Colombia's Green Growth Policy and its nationally determined contribution (NDC) show the Colombian government's commitment to a low-carbon, climate-resilient future (CNPD 2019; Colombia 2020). The Green Growth Policy aims to drive a national, climate-compatible increase in productivity and economic competitiveness by 2030, while ensuring social inclusion and sustainable use of the country's natural wealth. The policy sets out a framework for integrating efforts toward environmental sustainability in sectoral policies and economic growth strategies and also provides a road map for the transition to an economic model based on green growth.

Regarding Colombia's NDC, under the Paris Agreement the country commits to reduce its greenhouse gas emissions by 20 percent (relative to a projected business-as-usual scenario) by 2030. Additional adaptation measures outlined in the NDC include (1) the incorporation of adaptation and resilience considerations in sectoral, spatial, and development planning; (2) water resource management tools for the country's priority water basins; (3) delimitation and protection of Colombia's high mountain Andean ecosystems; (4) establishment of additional protected areas; and (5) inclusion of climate change considerations in sectoral planning (with an emphasis on agriculture) and in strategic national projects.

The downturn has also drawn heavily on government coffers even as revenues dropped. A government stimulus spending program to address COVID-19 is equivalent to about 10 percent of GDP nationally, making it one of the highest levels of government expenditure in Latin America (after Brazil) (World Bank 2020, figure 6). The impacts of COVID-19 have been particularly acute among the Wayuu, an indigenous group in Colombia and bordering República Bolivariana de Venezuela. A report by Human Rights Watch and the Johns Hopkins Center for Humanitarian Health observes that "the pandemic and lockdown are making it harder than ever for the Wayuu, many of whom live in the Colombian northeastern department of La Guajira, to get adequate food, water, and health care at a time when they need them more than ever" (HRW 2020). Moreover, the country has seen a massive influx of more than 1.8 million Venezuelan migrants, putting additional pressure on its public services (OECD 2019).

Coal is currently the second most important export in the national economy, and Colombian coal production represents 8 percent of the global market (Cerrejón 2020). In 2019 Cerrejón provided the Colombian government US$534 million in taxes and royalties, accounting for 0.65 percent of the national budget and 23.0 percent of Colombia's total mining revenue (Cerrejón 2020).

REGIONAL CONTEXT

The department of La Guajira in northeastern Colombia comprises most of the Guajira Peninsula and is bordered by the Caribbean Sea and, to the south, by República Bolivariana de Venezuela. La Guajira is the most ethnically diverse department in the country; indigenous groups—primarily the Wayuu people—and Afro-Colombians represent nearly 60 percent of the department's total population. The department suffers from the highest rates of poverty, child mortality, and illiteracy in Colombia and has severe deficiencies in human capital and physical and social infrastructure (CNPD 2019). The local economy is heavily dependent on the Cerrejón mine, while most of the population relies on subsistence agriculture. La Guajira contributes only 1 percent of Colombia's agricultural production and accounts for only 1.3 percent of the planted area of the country (CCG 2018). There is very little crop irrigation, and most of the agriculture is located in the southern area of the department, where water resources are more available.

The Guajira Peninsula has been identified as one of Colombia's regions most vulnerable to climate variability and with one of the highest water deficits (Iagua 2014). Physical conditions are harsh, with high temperatures, strong winds, and frequent droughts. An extended drought during 2012–16, linked to the El Niño phenomenon, led to famine in the region, with elevated levels of child mortality due to undernutrition (Contreras et al. 2020). High levels of immigration from República Bolivariana de Venezuela have exacerbated socioeconomic challenges within the department. And while the peace accord of 2016 has markedly improved the security situation, organized armed groups associated with drug trafficking remain active in the region and exacerbate social instability.[2]

At the same time, La Guajira has been identified as one of Colombia's highest potential areas for solar and wind energy production and has considerable tourism potential, given its rugged coastline, high coastal and marine biodiversity, excellent conditions for sports such as kite surfing, bird watching, and rich cultural heritage.

MINE CONTEXT

The Cerrejón mining operation, comprising a large open-pit coal mine plus a rail line and seaport, is a joint venture between Anglo American, BHP, and Glencore. The mine, shown in photo 1.1, is the largest in Latin America and one of the largest coal mining operations in the world, employing more than 6,000 direct employees. Operated since 1985, the mine's current lease runs until 2033, with closure planned in 2034.

The Cerrejón mine offers relatively high salaries and plays a central role in the economy of La Guajira. The vast majority of the mine's 6,000 employees are from La Guajira or neighboring departments. At the same time, the presence and activities of the large-scale mine in the context of the high-poverty, environmentally fragile department have sparked social conflict over the years. Local communities and civil society groups have mounted protests, accusing the mine of causing human rights abuses and air pollution, among other issues. Worker protests, relating to employment terms and conditions, have led to prolonged strikes and stoppages.

To help address some of the region's challenges, the Cerrejón mine has undertaken numerous local socioeconomic development initiatives. In 2019, the mine (either directly or through the Cerrejón Foundation) invested more than US$3.7 million in social programs such as capacity building of local organizations or interventions to improve access to water,

PHOTO 1.1
Cerrejón mine

Source: © Dobbin International. Used with the permission of Dobbin International. Further permission required for reuse.

particularly in Upper Guajira, as well as providing scholarships and educational aid to local students (Cerrejón 2020). The mine has been implementing natural resource conservation programs, including the creation of a biological corridor linking the Sierra Nevada de Santa Marta and Montes de Oca forests, which has resulted in the return of the jaguar to this area (Cerrejón 2020).

GEOGRAPHIC SCOPE

The geographic scope for the strategic spatial development planning was determined in the early stages of the work, following initial analysis of the biophysical patterns and administrative organization of the area. The scope encompasses not only the immediate area around the Cerrejón mine but the extent of La Guajira Department, while also taking into account the wider regional and national context. In addition, the report includes the adjacent coastal and marine zones along the 600 kilometers of coastline to a depth of 200 meters (see map 1.1). Map 1.1 shows the terrestrial boundaries of the department, which includes 15 municipalities and covers approximately 21,000 square kilometers. Box 1.2 describes how an application of the spatial development planning approach for a mining project in Guinea focused sequentially on different geographic scopes, encompassing national, regional, and prefecture levels.

MAP 1.1

Geographic scope of the planning work: The department of La Guajira

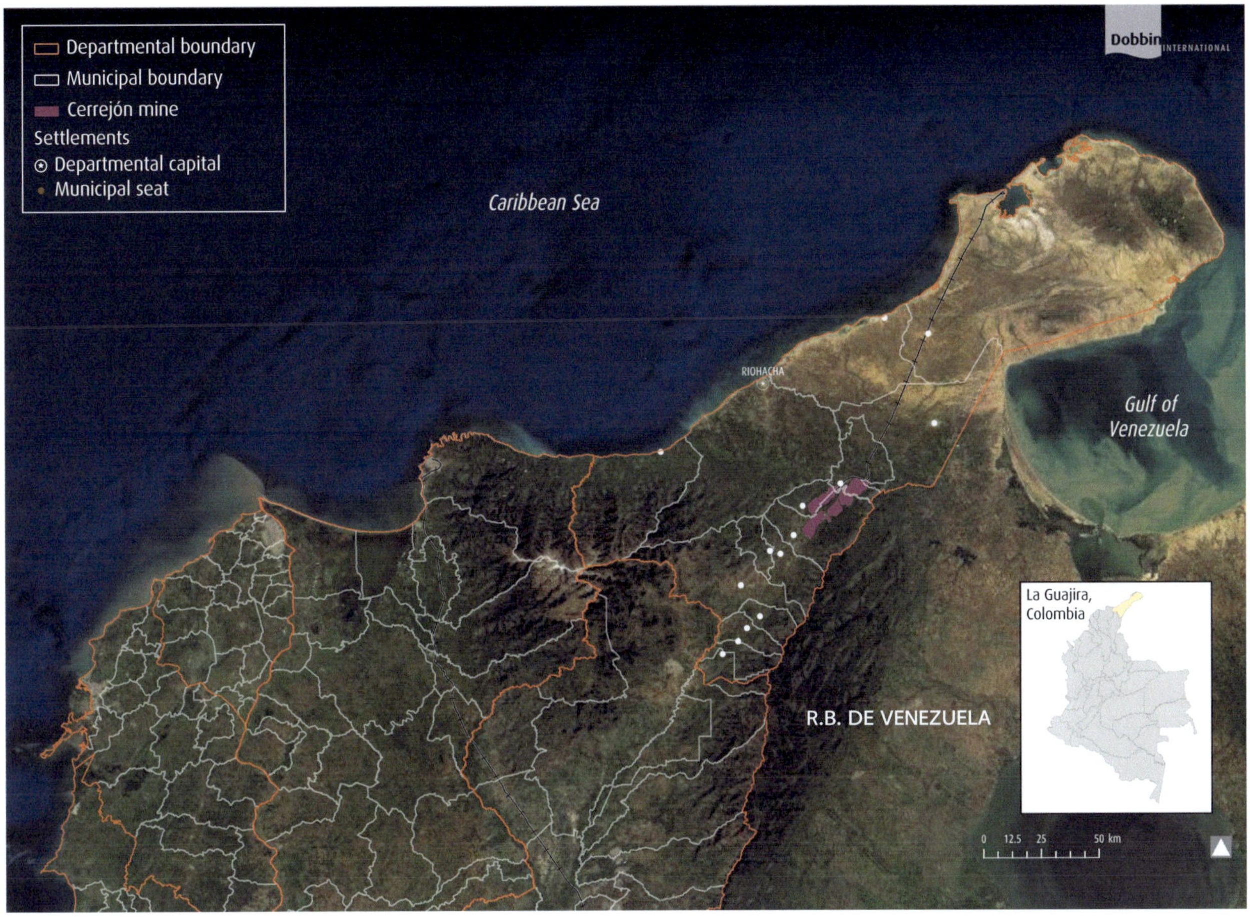

Source: Dobbin International 2020, using data from Esri, DigitalGlobe, GeoEye, Earthstar Geographics, CNES/Airbus DS, US Department of Agriculture, US Geological Survey, AeroGRID, IGN, and the GIS user community.

BOX 1.2

Strategic spatial development planning in Guinea: A multiscale approach

Envisaged as the largest integrated mine, rail, and port project in the world, Rio Tinto's Simandou project in Guinea was anticipated to provide not only massive direct contributions to the Guinean economy but also even larger opportunities to catalyze the country's economic and social development. Rio Tinto commissioned Dobbin International (DI) to develop a national strategic spatial development plan to build a vision for Guinea's future based on leveraging Rio Tinto's core investments in physical and social infrastructure for multisector broad-based growth and development.

The planning team worked at a number of different scales during the planning process. National-level analysis was needed to define the region based on biophysical and socioeconomic factors and to identify connections and opportunities with other countries in West Africa. In defining the regional development corridor that would be created by Rio Tinto's investments, the planning team took a multithematic view of the underlying social, cultural, administrative, biological, physical, and economic conditions in the region—far from the typical approach of looking at a narrow swath of land adjacent to a road or rail line.

continued

Box 1.2, *continued*

After defining the Southern Guinean Growth Corridor, a 47,065-square-kilometer region associated with the planned 650-kilometer rail line, DI undertook a series of detailed spatial and economic analyses to gain better insights into the opportunities across all sectors (for example, agriculture, fisheries, forestry, and tourism). Through the use of DI's unique spatial planning and economic analysis process, the planning team identified approximately US$3 billion per year in economic potential in agriculture, forestry, and fisheries in five distinct regional planning zones within the growth corridor. Finally, a series of "deep dives" into the prefectures and subprefectures with the highest relevance to the project were undertaken, allowing for even more detailed analysis and a better understanding of the opportunities for broad-based growth and development. One of these deep dives focused on Forécariah Prefecture, as this was to be one of the two national economic hubs created by the mining project and would be one of the areas most affected by the project as the gateway to the new corridor.

DI's comprehensive planning process included targeted data development (including the creation of high-resolution land-use information from satellite imagery), spatial and economic modeling to complement the national-level work, and a strategic plan to guide future decisions and investments in the prefecture and region. The geospatial database developed as part of the project was designed to fit seamlessly into Rio Tinto's existing data infrastructure, allowing the work to provide guidance to environmental assessments, zoning, resettlement, and other future work.

The strategic plans identified four broad areas that can be distinguished across the prefecture for planning purposes: the vulnerable coast, an urban core, a commercial corridor, and a pastoral savannah. Economic analyses found that the prefecture's total economic potential is at least US$600 million per year (only including the primary sectors of agriculture, forestry, and fisheries), and up to US$3 billion per year (including also value-added processing, trade, and services sectors). If managed well, development of the prefecture—catalyzed by the Simandou project and other interventions—would enable this area to take full advantage of its strategic location and economic potential.

Sources: Dobbin International 2012a, 2012b; Rio Tinto 2013.

NOTES

1. See this chapter's section "Geographic Scope" for a description of the geographical extent of La Guajira Department.
2. There are numerous reports and articles on this topic. See, for example, Boraz (2007) and a recent report from the International Crisis Group (ICG 2020).

REFERENCES

Boraz, S. 2007. "Case Study: The Colombia-Venezuela Border." In *Ungoverned Territories: Understanding and Reducing Terrorism Risks,* edited by Angel Rabasa, Steven Boraz, Peter Chalk, Kim Cragin, Theodore W. Karasik, Jennifer D. P. Moroney, Kevin A. O'Brien, and John E. Peters, 243–76. Santa Monica, CA: Rand Corporation. https://www.jstor.org/stable/10.7249/mg561af.20?seq=1#metadata_info_tab_contents.

CCG (Cámara de Comercio de la Guajira). 2018. *Informe Socioeconómico de la Guajira: Estudio Sobre el Desempeño Económico Territorial 2017.* Riohacha, La Guardia: Cámara de Comercio de la Guajira. http://www.camaraguajira.org/publicaciones/informes/estudio-economico-de-la-guajira-2017.pdf.

Cerrejón. 2020. *Cerrejón's Sustainability Report 2019*. Albania, La Guajira: Cerrejón. https://www.cerrejon.com/wp-content/uploads/CERREJ%C3%93NS-SUSTAINABILITY-REPORT_2019.pdf.

CNPD (Colombia National Planning Department). 2019. "Green Growth Policy." CONPES Document 3934 of 2018, Council for Social and Economic Policy, Bogotá DC, Colombia. https://www.dnp.gov.co/Crecimiento-Verde/Documents/Pol%C3%ADtica%20CONPES%203934/Executive%20Summary%20Green%20Growth%20Policy.pdf.

Colombia. 2020. First Nationally Determined Contributions, Updated Submission. December 29, 2020. NDC Registry, UNFCC. https://www4.unfccc.int/sites/NDCStaging/pages/Party.aspx?party=COL.

Contreras, D., A. Voets, J. Junghardt, S. Bhamidipati, and S. Contreras. 2020. "The Drivers of Child Mortality during the 2012–2016 Drought in La Guajira, Colombia." *International Journal of Disaster Risk Science* 11: 87–104. https://link.springer.com/article/10.1007/s13753-020-00255-0.

Dobbin International. 2012a. *Guinea: Passage from Poverty to Prosperity—How Visionary Development Can Transform a Country from Poverty to Prosperity*. Report prepared for Rio Tinto SIMFER SA. Herndon, VA: Dobbin International.

Dobbin International. 2012b. *Guinea: Forécariah–Simandou's Coastal Gateway*. Report prepared for Rio Tinto SIMFER SA. Herndon, VA: Dobbin International.

Dobbin International. 2020. *Strategy for Sustainable and Resilient Development of La Guajira, Colombia*. Report prepared for Cerrejón mine. Herndon, VA: Dobbin International.

HRW (Human Rights Watch). 2020. "People of Resilience: Colombia's Wayuu Indigenous Community Confronts a Malnutrition Crisis Amid Covid-19." New York: Human Rights Watch. https://www.hrw.org/video-photos/interactive/2020/08/13/people-resilience-colombias-wayuu-indigenous-community.

Iagua. 2014. "El departamento de la Guajira es el más vulnerable de Colombia ante El Niño." Madrid: Iagua. https://www.iagua.es/noticias/colombia/ideam/14/12/10/departamento-guajira-es-mas-vulnerable-colombia-nino.

ICG (International Crisis Group). 2020. *Disorder on the Border: Keeping the Peace between Colombia and Venezuela*. Brussels: International Crisis Group. https://www.crisisgroup.org/latin-america-caribbean/andes/colombiavenezuela/84-disorder-border-keeping-peace-between-colombia-and-venezuela.

IPS (Inter Press Service News Agency). 2018. "Q&A: Greening Colombia's Energy Mix." IPS, June 6. http://www.ipsnews.net/2018/06/qa-greening-colombias-energy-mix/.

OECD (Organisation for Economic Co-operation and Development). 2019. "OECD Policy Note on the Venezuelan Migration Shock in Colombia and Its Fiscal Implications." Paris: OECD. https://www.oecd.org/economy/surveys/Colombia-migration-shock-note-english-2019.pdf.

Rio Tinto. 2013. *Simandou Economic Impact Report*. London: Rio Tinto. https://www.corporateregister.com/search/report.cgi?num=70369-BlZGpTQnzD6.

World Bank. 2020. *Colombia Resilient and Sustainable Infrastructure for Recovery DPF (P173424)*. September 2 (Public Disclosure Version). Washington, DC: World Bank. http://documents1.worldbank.org/curated/en/322661601776858403/pdf/Colombia-Resilient-and-Sustainable-Infrastructure-for-Recovery-Development-Policy-Financing-Project.pdf.

2 Methodology

THE PLANNING APPROACH

The strategic spatial development planning approach uses advanced geospatial planning tools and multisectoral analyses grounded in extensive collaboration to define green-growth-related issues, options, action plans, and potential investments at local and regional levels, taking into account national and international contexts and opportunities.

The core of the Dobbin International (DI) planning approach (see appendix A) is based on the concept that social, political, economic, and geographic realities, among others, interact in a given territory and must be analyzed jointly to obtain a full diagnosis and offer better guidance for decision-making. The tools used as the basis for these analyses include geospatial data compilation and database management, and initial and thematic-scenario-based spatial suitability models. These tools facilitate capturing and analyzing large volumes of georeferenced data and enable stakeholder discussions based on maps of these data. Maps and scenario development models, driven by science and data-driven spatial analysis, allow stakeholders to develop insights into current conditions and potential alternative futures. This integration of geospatial technology in creative problem-solving, now sometimes known as "geodesign,"[1] provides a significant evidence base for the decision-making process.

The planning approach considers a wide range of administrative, biophysical, environmental, social, and economic factors (current conditions and longer-term trends) that shape an area's development potential. Key concerns in preparing a strategic plan and identifying investment opportunities are

- The sustainable management and/or rehabilitation of the area's natural resource base for productive uses; and
- The development of an integrated set of multisectoral investments (for example, in agriculture, forestry, tourism, energy, infrastructure, and urban development) that take full advantage of potential cross-sectoral synergies.

The planning approach has often been used in the context of large-scale mining operations to develop a framework of potential initiatives that can be implemented by the concerned mining companies, other actors (such as the private sector, the government, or nongovernmental organizations [NGOs]), or through multistakeholder collaborative programs.

The planning team examined the region and department's natural resource base from a systems-based, spatial analysis perspective, combining expert analyses, stakeholder consultations, field assessments, and professional interpretation of spatial patterns and trends revealed by the use of satellite imagery and other maps. Thematic-scenario-based spatial suitability models were produced, covering the most promising sectors and taking advantage of the multisectoral synergies identified. These scenarios considered existing and potentially new economic drivers (such as agriculture, forest plantations, livestock production, fishery and mariculture, tourism, alternative uses of mining infrastructure, oil and gas, and renewable energy) as well as support drivers (including conservation, restoration, urban development, and infrastructure) needed to underpin green growth in the department.

Following the spatial analyses and working with the management of the mine and a wide range of other stakeholders, the research team developed a strategic plan for the department to realize its green growth opportunities. This process involved the following:

- Identifying distinct planning zones, each with a relatively homogeneous set of biophysical characteristics
- Conducting economic analyses to show alternative futures for La Guajira
- Preparing a project bank of prioritized initiatives for implementation by the various economic actors involved (the private sector, including Cerrejón, the government, NGOs, and so forth).

LINKS WITH THE GREEN GROWTH FRAMEWORK

The planning approach complements the green growth framework, as set out in a recent World Bank report (Sekar et al. 2019), and extends its application to a broader set of issues. While the planning approach predates the concepts of green growth and the green growth framework, it is predicated on the same shared principle that mining operations can play a catalytic role in finding innovative ways to leverage natural resource wealth for broad-based, climate-proofed economic growth while maintaining healthy, productive ecosystems. The recent World Bank report on the green growth framework focuses on three areas where the mining industry has been or can be an engine of change for green growth: namely, renewable energy, water management, and physical infrastructure. The planning approach described in this study incorporates all of these areas while also considering innovative green approaches for key economic sectors such as agriculture, forestry, fisheries, and tourism. In addition, the strategic spatial plan focuses on activities essential to supporting economic development, including the restoration of landscapes and water resources and conservation (wise management of land and coastal and marine zones).

The green growth framework categorizes three types of climate-sensitive mining initiatives undertaken by mining companies: those related to compliance, to resource planning, and to local value creation. These three categories can be enhanced using the strategic spatial development planning approach (see table 2.1).

TABLE 2.1 **Strategic spatial development planning links with the green growth framework**

GREEN GROWTH FRAMEWORK (GGF)		STRATEGIC SPATIAL DEVELOPMENT PLANNING: RELEVANCE TO GGF	STRATEGIC SPATIAL DEVELOPMENT PLANNING: EXPANSION OF GGF
Climate-sensitive mining initiatives	Compliance	Medium/high	Medium
	Resource planning	High	Strong
	Local value creation	High	Strong

Source: Original table for this publication.

In terms of compliance-related initiatives, the planning approach offers mining companies a structured means of aligning with government policies and external requirements or standards regarding, for example, local content, and certain aspects of social and environmental performance and mine closure.[2]

In terms of resource planning, there is an important difference between the planning approach described here and the initiatives covered in the green growth framework. The framework relates to mining companies' investments in green infrastructure or technologies with the primary goal of making their operations more resource efficient or climate sensitive, and with secondary development gains in terms of boosting employment, skills, and supply chains. By contrast, the strategic spatial development planning approach takes as its starting point that mining companies have a direct interest in supporting broad-based sustainable development in the regions where they operate. There are many different ways in which companies can look beyond their own operational investments to leverage their activities and their resources to support natural-resource-based development. For example, mine sites with large workforces can create sufficient demand for food products to warrant high-value-adding investments in agriculture and agroprocessing, while mines' rail or port infrastructure can be redesigned for shared use to facilitate wider market access for such products.

Finally, there is a difference between the planning approach and the "local value creation" category of initiatives in the green growth framework. Such initiatives are characterized as attempts by mining firms to "add local value through local procurement, employment, and regional planning efforts to comply with local content regulation or to secure their long-term social license to operate with local stakeholders" (Sekar et al. 2019, 3). As described in a recent World Bank report, these are "typically climate-agnostic activities or activities reflecting corporate social responsibility that are too bespoke and limited in scale to offer any real catalytic effect" (Sekar et al. 2019, 3). Numerous applications of the planning approach have shown that this perceived limitation does not always hold for regional planning efforts, for three reasons:

- First, planning for local value creation can go hand in hand with planning scalable investments that create broad-based green growth (for example, in agriculture).
- Second, the strategic spatial development planning approach can be conducted at different scales, from national to regional to department. Even when used at a local level, the planning focuses on scalable investments that connect with external market opportunities for greater impact.
- Third, climate-sensitive planning is central to the approach, which takes a conservative perspective on climate vulnerabilities, planning for low-carbon high-value investments that build resilience to future climate conditions.

The strategic spatial development planning approach effectively pushes the boundaries of the green growth framework to encompass the identification and planning of scalable climate-sensitive investments related—either directly or indirectly—to mining operations and offering high-value potential for green growth.

THE GREEN GROWTH APPROACH USED IN THIS CASE STUDY

The planning work in La Guajira initially focused on economic diversification for the mining-dependent department, using the well-established multisectoral and resource-based approach. Then, during the planning process, the concept of green growth became an explicit part of the collaborative discussions with the Cerrejón mine. The strategic plan for the department of La Guajira, grounded as it is in environmental conservation and restoration, renewable energy, ecotourism, and wise resource management, became referred to as the "green growth strategy." Cerrejón also had an interest in the concept as it aligns well with the company's sustainability strategy, which includes initiatives in, for example, reforestation, biodiversity conservation, and improvements in water infrastructure (Cerrejón 2020). In addition, the planning team sought to identify synergies with Colombia's national green growth strategy. Exploration of the connections among the planning approach, the green growth framework, and Colombia's green growth strategy led to development of this case study.

Furthermore, there is a clear need to plan for postclosure from the earliest stage possible in order to lessen the economic and social shock to this mining-dependent department. This is particularly important given that key European export markets for Colombia's thermal coal are phasing out their coal use as part of efforts to accelerate green growth and climate action (New Climate Institute 2018).[3] Planning for post mine closure was also an important objective of the planning work (box 2.1).

BOX 2.1

Planning beyond mine closure

The planning work considered a 2034 mine closure as a base-case scenario and proposed high-value-added investments that would generate significant employment and economic benefits to strengthen the department's resilience and mitigate the worst socioeconomic impacts of closure. The need to plan for the department's transition away from coal mining is underlined by the fact that this mining-dependent area has few other major industries present, making it highly vulnerable to the problems highlighted in a recent World Bank report on coal mine closure (World Bank 2018). The strategic plan developed for La Guajira directly addresses regional economic diversification and rejuvenation by setting out a clear road map for job creation and private sector development beyond coal mining, to be implemented through collaborative efforts involving the government, private sector, civil society, and other economic actors. On the other hand, technical, environmental, and social issues associated with the phasing out of coal mining and a just transition for its workers and related industries are outside the scope of the La Guajira strategic spatial development strategy and plan and are not discussed in this report.

PHASED APPROACH

The planning, which took place over a nine-month period in 2019–20, followed the spatial development planning methodology developed by DI, consisting of three distinct phases (see appendix A). These phases, each requiring approximately three months' work, include the following:

- *Phase 1: Compilation of spatial and nonspatial data.* A database of relevant spatial and nonspatial data was compiled and managed to form the basis for the spatial and economic analyses. Data were sourced from the mining operations as well as statistical information, reports, and other documents from government agencies, NGOs, university databases, and others. Data on land use and land cover were obtained from 2019 satellite imagery CORINE[4] land-cover analysis.
- *Phase 2: Spatial and economic analysis of opportunities and constraints.* Analyses of biophysical, environmental, and socioeconomic conditions and trends (for example, poverty, immigration, water availability, land degradation, pollution, and environmentally sensitive areas) led to the identification of opportunities for new initiatives and investments (in ecotourism, innovative agricultural production, forestry, and other areas).
- *Phase 3: Development of a strategic action plan.* A green growth strategy for the department of La Guajira was articulated, including action plans for integrated investments and institutional arrangements for their implementation.

A fourth phase—implementation of the strategic plan—is built into the methodology. In some cases, this may involve a multistakeholder platform, whereas in other cases a more formal arrangement may be more appropriate, such as an independent (nongovernmental) institution with convening power to coordinate detailed planning, implementation, and monitoring.

FIELD ASSESSMENTS

On-the-ground investigations and the use of satellite imagery are essential elements of the approach. In La Guajira, these involved the following:

- Several road trips to traverse the department in 4x4 vehicles, to see firsthand, WBS the state of the road network and to check realistic travel times between different areas as part of the accessibility assessment
- Travel by light aircraft at a height of 500 meters, in order to reach remote areas and to better understand the different ecosystems, patterns of population density and distribution, land use and land cover, degraded lands, and high potential lands (The flyover also gave a very useful overview of the department's water sources, seasonal rivers, coastal lagoons, coastal erosion, salt flats, and marine resources.)
- Travel by boat, thanks to gracious support from the Colombian coast guard team stationed in La Guajira, to see something of the department's 600-kilometer coastline, which presents important opportunities for tourism (By sea it was also possible to clearly see the need for improvements in the existing port infrastructure to better facilitate local producers' access to outside markets.)

COLLABORATION: EMBEDDED IN THE PLANNING APPROACH

Rather than being an add-on feature of the strategic spatial development planning approach, collaboration is an integral characteristic without which the approach would not be possible. This DI collaborative approach was also used in the context of Anglo American's mining operations in Limpopo, South Africa, and was termed by the company as "collaborative regional development." Boxes 2.2, 2.3, 4.1, and 5.2 illustrate the process of using geospatial data and planning processes for collaborative regional development. Maps, derived from the advanced geospatial analyses and planning, are key to the collaborative approach, as they enable a focused and productive discussion of future options and decisions.

Across all applications of the approach, collaboration is integral throughout the process, with frequent rounds of discussion and joint development of a shared vision for the future of the area or region around the mine. These dialogues involve a wide range of stakeholders, including, at the minimum, the planning team, relevant staff of the mining companies involved, and government agencies, as well as other experts, other organizations operating in the area, and representatives of local communities. In addition, formal workshops are held at key points in the process:

- A *kick-off meeting* prior to the start of planning, to discuss objectives and expectations and to prepare for a smooth process
- A *data review workshop* following phase 1, to address any data gaps or discrepancies and identify the need for any further sourcing of specific data

BOX 2.2

Dobbin International (DI) use of Spatial Delphi technique for collaborative regional planning

In other applications of the strategic spatial development planning approach, DI has used the well-known Spatial Delphi decision-making system to facilitate participatory planning. In this approach, the DI planning team first invites different stakeholders from across the planning region to participate in workshops and breakout sessions. Collaboratively, this joint team identifies priorities in dealing with conservation, development, and climate resilience. These issues touch on infrastructure, landscape degradation, water availability, connectivity, employment, and so on. Next, all the experts are asked to rank the importance of these priorities and outline spatial strategies to address them. A series of suitability analyses with geospatial data are conducted on site during a workshop to visualize these spatial strategies and options with maps created "on the fly."

For example, a suitability map of conservation will identify the best and worst areas for conservation. The resulting series of maps will be overlaid based on the ranking to reveal consensus and conflict among the different interest groups in the team. All the participants will be asked to read the outcome overlays of maps, then conduct multiple rounds of ranking and refinement of spatial strategies. This approach allows the exchange of knowledge and information among people with different sets of expertise. Potential conflicts of interest can be presented clearly by maps with rankings and criteria, which will enable focused discussions and help planners, planning authorities, and local communities make evidence-based decisions.

BOX 2.3

Getting collaboration right from the start: An example from Madagascar

In 1999, when Madagascar QIT Minerals (QMM, a division of Rio Tinto) was seriously considering developing an ilmenite mine in the impoverished Anosy Region of Madagascar, QMM president Daniel Lambert noted that if "they were to be successful in their mining project, the region needed to be successful," and the company planned to support the region in achieving sustainable economic growth. QMM initiated and later partnered with the World Bank to support the preparation of a regional development strategy and action plan and Dobbin International (DI) was commissioned to undertake strategic spatial planning on behalf of the Anosy Region.

In the past, regional development planning in the Anosy Region had been done through largely unsuccessful top-down approaches undertaken by central government agencies. In this case, a new bottom-up spatial planning approach was suggested by DI, through the creation of a Committee for Regional Development (CRD) involving regional stakeholders in all aspects of the planning and decision-making process. The CRD served as an independent, nonpolitical platform for discussing, reviewing, and guiding the collaborative process and the development of an integrated regional development strategy and investment action plan across every sector in the region. The CRD comprised participants from the local business community, nongovernmental organizations, mayors, and other representatives of the 38 participating communes, and regionally based representatives of the national administration (ministries of mines, agriculture, environment, education, transportation, tourism, and so forth). James Dobbin, president and CEO of DI, acted as chief technical adviser to the CRD, advising the executive of the CRD and leading the local CRD Malagasy technical team and international expert team during a five-year period (1999–2004).

A critical component of the regional planning approach was the development of a geospatial database (using geographical information system technology) and the introduction to the team and CRD of spatial information management, spatial analysis, and spatial strategies and technologies including remote sensing and strategic regional planning techniques. An issues-driven approach was used to bring stakeholders together to debate critical issues, such as environmental degradation, conservation, mining, and tourism and to define development options, scenarios, alternative futures, and strategies.

The Anosy project was a striking example of how regional and local economic development and mining can have strong synergies. One of the major obstacles to developing the mine was the financing of a port, as the mining company would not be able to undertake the whole investment itself—making the mine not feasible. Through the regional planning process (with the involvement of Rio Tinto), a broader (and participative) regional analysis and plan clearly showed that many sectors need the port and that a multiuse port could substantially influence the economic development of the region and the nation.

The 20-year Regional Development Framework (RDF) action plan was developed through this highly collaborative approach. The RDF encouraged donors to invest in this impoverished region. Among others, the World Bank decided to include the Fort-Dauphin region as one of its three "growth poles" for the development of Madagascar with a US$300 million investment—with US$60 million of this going to finance the multiuse port in partnership with Rio Tinto (US$60 million each). Some US$500 million of the US$715 million RDF plan was already committed in the first year of the Anosy region's 20-year development plan.

Sources: Dobbin International 1999, 2001, 2004; Dobbin International and CRD de l'Anosy 2001–05; Landscapes/Paysages 2008. See also the World Bank's collection of documentation for the Integrated Growth Poles Project for Madagascar, "Integrated Growth Poles," https://projects.worldbank.org/en/projects-operations/project-detail/P083351?lang=en, and "MG—Integrated Growth Poles Additional Financing Credit," https://projects.worldbank.org/en/projects-operations/project-detail/P110405?lang=en&tab=overview.

- A *second review workshop* following phase 2, to discuss the analyses and the identified opportunities and constraints
- A *final workshop* after phase 3, to review in detail the strategic plan, the specific project plans, and the mechanisms for their implementation

In the case of La Guajira, detailed consultations were carried out before the start of the spatial planning work and are summarized in a document titled "Prospective Agenda for La Guajira." Launched in 2016 by a group of stakeholders (the United Nations Development Programme, the government of La Guajira, the National Federation of Departments, the National Learning Service—SENA, the Regional Autonomous Corporation of La Guajira, the Chamber of Commerce of La Guajira, Cerrejón's Foundation for Institutional Strengthening, and the Cerrejón's Guajira Indigenous Foundation), this initiative undertook extensive dialogue and consultations with citizens in order to sketch out a road map that would lead to a large work agreement to build the department's future. An initial exercise was conducted by key actors in order to identify the current situation in La Guajira. Additional discussions were convened to identify desired targets capable of being attained and to establish the main courses of action to achieve them. Ideal scenarios were built for La Guajira's future, prioritizing three strategic lines in education, promotion of a multicultural society, and development of a new economy. In order to understand the perceptions and expectations of the local population, household surveys were also conducted (Trust 2016). The initiative spurred considerable uptake from local think tanks, academia, and the regional government, which hosted regular debates and follow-up initiatives. The agenda's key priorities include the following:

- Define a Departmental Master Plan for La Guajira.
- Identify and prioritize the department's needs going forward, alongside the national government and its institutions.
- Strengthen the culture of caring for public infrastructure.
- Promote economic activities, leveraging preexisting vocations.
- Define an inclusive economic vision for La Guajira that benefits all communities.
- Reactivate and strengthen trade relationships with the greater Caribbean and República Bolivariana de Venezuela.
- Develop local capacities for the management of innovation processes and entrepreneurship.
- Promote heritage and cultural resources in the department.
- Define opportunities for intercultural dialogue.
- Promote equitable access to education for all the inhabitants of the department.
- Meet minimum quality standards for schools and teachers.
- Strengthen the social fabric in the department.
- Promote the sustainable use of natural resources.

To inform the spatial planning work described in this report, additional consultations were carried out involving over 100 organizations and individuals, through individual meetings, focus group discussions, and larger meetings in Bogotá and in the department. These consultations revealed almost universal recognition of the need to strengthen coordination of different stakeholders' efforts and interventions in the department, and support for planning the transition from the current mining-dependent economy to one based on diverse, multisectoral green growth.

NOTES

1. Geodesign is a collaborative and multidisciplinary approach to designing and realizing the optimal solutions for spatial challenges in the built and natural environments, often using geospatial technologies and data in an integrated planning process. See Steinitz (2012) for a detailed description of this approach.
2. The spatial planning methodology presented in this report can be used to assess land management and repurposing options, making it a complement to the mine closure and just transition toolbox. A recent World Bank (2018) report provides a comprehensive discussion of the technical, environmental, and social aspects of coal mine closure.
3. Cerrejón, one of Colombia's largest coal producers, has turned to alternative markets, such as Turkey, but has nonetheless suffered from the shrinking market and lowered price of coal (Cerrejón 2020).
4. Better known by its acronym, in full it is Coordination of Information on the Environment (European Union program).

REFERENCES

Cerrejón. 2020. *Cerrejón's Sustainability Report 2019*. Albania, La Guajira: Cerrejón. https://www.cerrejon.com/wp-content/uploads/CERREJ%C3%93NS-SUSTAINABILITY-REPORT_2019.pdf.

Dobbin International. 1999. *The Fort-Dauphin Region: Coastal Zone Management Issues and Port Site Selection Options*. Report prepared for Madagascar QIT Minerals (QMM), Rio Tinto, Montreal, Quebec. Herndon, VA: Dobbin International.

Dobbin International. 2001. *Fort-Dauphin Port Development: Preliminary Economic Analysis of Existing and Potential Port Use*. Prepared for Madagascar QIT Minerals (QMM), Rio Tinto, Montreal, Canada. Herndon, VA: Dobbin International.

Dobbin International. 2004. *Anosy Region: Estimated Benefits Associated with a Proposed US$30 Million Investment in Agriculture Adjacent to Fort-Dauphin*. Report prepared for the World Bank funded by Rio Tinto (QMM), Montreal, Canada. Herndon, VA: Dobbin International.

Dobbin International and CRD (Comité Régional de Développement) de l'Anosy. 2001–05. *Anosy: Schéma de développement régional (SDR)—Rapport de la Phase 2: Diagnostics préliminaires, Rapport de la Phase 3: Collecte d'informations pertinentes, Rapport de la Phase 4: Analyses—Les Grandes Orientations pour le Développement de la Région, Rapport de la Phase 5: Synthesis—Schema de Developpement Regional (SDR) de l'Anosy*. A series of four reports prepared for the CRD de l'Anosy, Fort-Dauphin, Madagascar. Herndon, VA: Dobbin International.

Landscapes/Paysages. 2008. "Madagascar: Unlocking the Potential." Interview with James Dobbin in *Landscapes/Paysages Magazine* 10 (4): https://www.csla-aapc.ca/sites/csla-aapc.ca/files/Landscape%20Paysages/Fall2008_0.PDF.

New Climate Institute. 2018. *Implementation of Nationally Determined Contributions: Colombia Country Report*. Climate Change 25/2018 Environmental Research of the Federal Ministry for the Environment, Nature Conservation and Nuclear Safety. Dessau-Roßlau, Germany: Umweltbundesamt. https://www.umweltbundesamt.de/sites/default/files/medien/1410/publikationen/2018-11-01_climate-change_25-2018_country-report-colombia.pdf.

Sekar, S., K. Lundin, C. Tucker, J. Figueiredo, S. Tordo, and J. Aguilar. 2019. *Building Resilience: A Green Growth Framework for Mobilizing Mining Investment*. International Development in Focus. Washington, DC: World Bank. doi:10.1596/978-1-4648-1426-6.

Steinitz, C. 2012. *A Framework for Geodesign: Changing Geography by Design*. Redlands, CA: Esri Press.

Trust. 2016. "Agenda prospectiva para La Guajira." Bogotá: Trust. http://guajira360.org/wp-content/uploads/2017/07/Agenda-Prospectiva-para-La-Guajira-La-Guajira-que-queremos-Ajustado.pdf.

World Bank. 2018. *Managing Coal Mine Closure: Achieving a Just Transition for All*. Washington, DC: World Bank. https://openknowledge.worldbank.org/handle/10986/31020.

3 Key Outputs in Developing the Spatial Analyses and Scenarios

CREATION OF THE DATABASE

The main output of the initial phase of data collection was a database of spatial and nonspatial data. The compiled nonspatial data amounted to more than 140 documents ranging from national policies and local development plans to sector-specific reports and statistics.

The compilation, organization, and management of the spatial database was a challenge. Most of the spatial data were not up to date, were unreliable, and were scattered among various institutions, agencies, and the private sector. Spatial data were sourced from government agencies (for example, on biophysical and demographic variables), international organizations (for example, on climate-change-related variables), and the mining operations (for example, on mining infrastructure and zones). In addition, the planning team generated additional spatial data in the form of up-to-date land-use and land-cover maps based on the interpretation of recent satellite imagery, spatial analysis models, dasymetric models of population distribution, and spatial data collected during field visits. The final structure of the spatial database is shown in appendix B and gives an indication of the scope and detail included. Covering a wide range of data on the main economic, biophysical, and environmental themes and sectors, the database also includes sociocultural data such as locations of indigenous reservations (which make up a significant part of the department), sacred sites, areas of cultural importance, and educational and health facilities.

DEVELOPMENT OF INITIAL SPATIAL ANALYSES

Drawing on the database, the planning team first developed an initial set of spatial analyses, which entailed significant recalibration and reclassification of data from different sources to combine related variables in composite spatial analysis maps on key environmental, social, and economic issues (see figure 3.1). These analyses revealed important opportunities for green growth, such as the

FIGURE 3.1

Scope of initial spatial analyses

Environmental analysis
- Water availability model
- Hydrographic zoning
- Environmentally sensitive areas
- Environmental vulnerability analysis
- Vulnerability and deforestation
- Climate change

Social analysis
- Population and distribution
- Population: in-migration
- Multiculturalism
- Poverty analysis

Economic analysis
- Solar energy potential
- Wind energy potential
- Wi-Fi and cell phone coverage
- Vehicular access
- Municipal added value

Source: Dobbin International 2020.

potential for improving water availability and restoring the landscape for productive activities.

One example of these initial spatial analyses that improves decision-making is the water availability model, shown in map 3.1. This map is based largely on groundwater maps that had been commissioned by Cerrejón mine some years previously but had not been used for development or conservation planning purposes. After sourcing the maps, the planning team completed additional analyses of the mine's hydrology maps to better understand the hydrological regime. La Guajira has the lowest level of rainfall in Colombia, and the population has suffered from high levels of water stress and frequent droughts over the years. Importantly, the planning team's lineament density analysis of the geological maps revealed that the northern section of the department, where water availability is lowest, has two large areas of high lineament density (the two purple areas in map 3.1), indicating multiple geological faults where water can infiltrate. The planning team thus identified, for the first time, the actual groundwater recharge areas and sources of the seasonal streams in the north and the perennial rivers in the south (the location of these sources is depicted by the pink shaded areas in map 3.1). By identifying these areas, the planning team was able to plan soil and water conservation initiatives to limit runoff, enable replenishment of groundwater resources, develop land and water restoration programs, and foresee productive use of the land for local communities.

Box 3.1 illustrates how strategic spatial development planning looks beyond the existing patterns of land use to identify high potential growth nodes and development corridors. Box 3.2 highlights the use of dasymetric analysis within this planning approach as a means to identify the poorest districts within a region.

MAP 3.1

Water availability and restoration

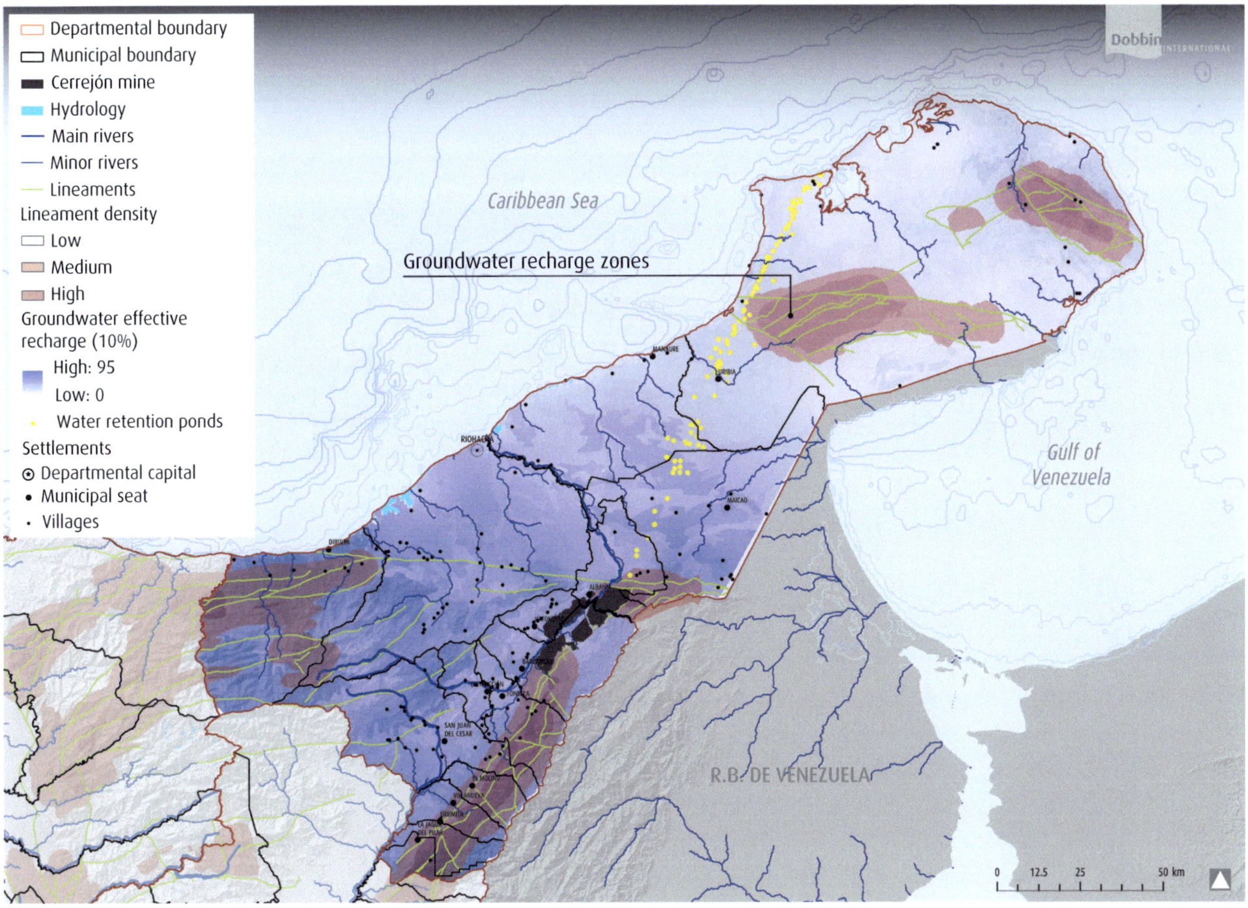

Source: Dobbin International 2020.

BOX 3.1

Mozambique: Identifying development potential beyond existing land-use patterns

Typical land-use planning undertaken by regions with limited budgets and narrow mandates will inevitably look for shortcuts and thereby tend to perpetuate existing land-use patterns that result in the same poverty index. In northern coastal Mozambique, for example, Dobbin International (DI) found, as a result of field surveys, review of satellite imagery, and spatial analysis of hydrological, river, and road systems, that the existing distribution of villages provided an inappropriate basis for land-use zoning for sustainable development. Existing land-settlement patterns were based on historical development: in colonial times engineers built roads on dry, sandy soils on the ridgelines (avoiding river valleys and wet areas) in order to reduce costs and extend the season for moving goods and people from landlocked areas to the coast. Eventually villages grew up along the road system as the civil war in the late twentieth century led people to escape from the interior toward the coast.

However, the most fertile lands for subsistence agriculture, and the most useful access points to good alluvial soils, with naturally growing large fruit trees and a little water in the streams even in the dry season, are not located where the roads were built. In most

continued

Box 3.1, *continued*

PHOTO B3.1.1

Area near Lichinga, Niassa Province, Mozambique

Source: © Dobbin International. Used with the permission of Dobbin International. Further permission required for reuse.

cases, these more fertile areas are 5 to 10 kilometers away from roads. Yet, still today, well-intentioned international agencies and nongovernmental organizations have been perpetuating these existing patterns of development by funding schools, clinics, and wells—keeping villagers in these unsustainable, extremely dry areas even though the best places for agriculture are along the river valleys.

DI has found similar development patterns in Guinea, Madagascar, Mozambique, South Africa, Tanzania, and elsewhere. One way to start rethinking the location of agricultural development or forestry initiatives is to look for places where roads and rivers meet. These crossings offer good access to markets, good water availability, and good alluvial soils. Developing land-based livelihood opportunities along either or both sides of river corridors can be much more effective than just focusing on road corridors.

Photo B3.1.1 and map B3.1.1 show the same area near Lichinga, Niassa Province, Mozambique. The blue areas of the map, where there is little or no productive activity, were found to be highly suitable for agricultural cropping and forest plantation based on DI's spatial suitability models. By contrast, the dark brown areas of the map show the dry sandy soil of the ridgelines where roads are located and where current agricultural activities are concentrated.

continued

Box 3.1, *continued*

MAP B3.1.1

Highest suitability areas for agriculture and forest plantation in Lichinga, Niassa Province, Mozambique

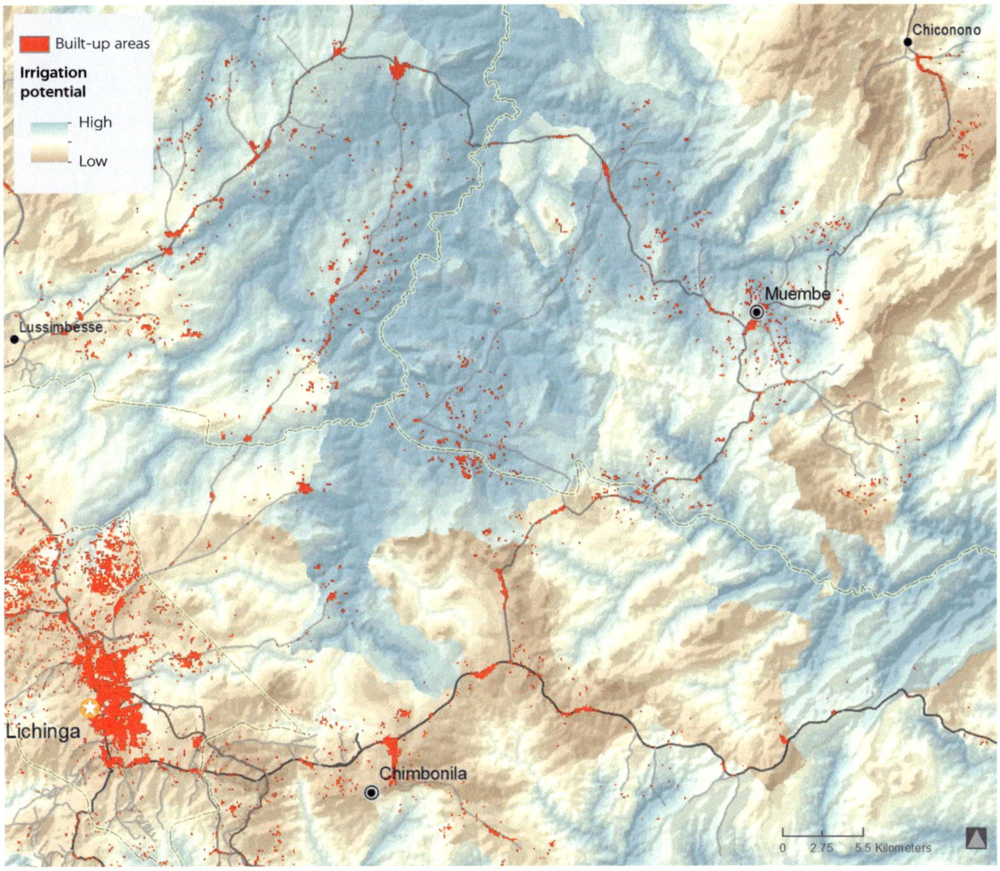

Sources: Dobbin International 2020.

Sources: Dobbin International 2007, 2010, 2013a, 2013b, 2013c, 2015–18; US Geological Survey et al. 2006; World Bank 2006.

DEVELOPMENT OF THEMATIC SCENARIOS

The initial spatial analysis maps, together with the insights gained from stakeholder discussions and field assessments, then served as the basis for identification of key constraints and opportunities for the development of La Guajira department. Additional spatial analyses and modeling were then conducted to prepare potential scenarios for developing the opportunities while taking into account the constraints identified in the initial spatial analysis scenarios. The thematic scenarios covered the following sectors:

- *Agriculture.* Spatial analyses included detailed agricultural suitability models for 16 different crops as well as the identification of multicropping areas where nine or more crops could be grown at the highest levels of suitability.

BOX 3.2

Strategic spatial development planning to identify areas of extreme poverty

Spatial analyses can reveal important social parameters to inform development planning. For example, in analyses performed for the World Bank's Systematic Country Diagnostic of Mozambique (an analysis of development opportunities and constraints), the planning team undertook a novel poverty-mapping approach based on dasymetric modeling. This is a spatial analysis model developed by Dobbin International that shows precisely where people are located—from their "footprints" on the ground, rather than relying on population distribution by administrative units. By integrating this modeling with poverty maps based on the United Nations Human Development Index, World Bank poverty mapping, and World Bank household survey data, the planning team was able to identify the 14 poorest districts out of the 156 districts in Mozambique. This technique provided clear guidance as to the geographic places where World Bank support should be focused. The World Bank's traditional poverty mapping approach can be enhanced with this new approach based on a composite of statistical and spatial data analyzed in different ways.

Sources: Dobbin International 2015; World Bank 2016.

The analyses built in climate change projections as of 2030 and no-go zones (including environmentally sensitive areas) to develop conservative estimates of agricultural production.

- *Agricultural processing centers.* Spatial analysis identified the most suitable locations for agricultural processing centers by considering variables such as proximity to administrative centers, urban settlements, main roads, and railroads (as the analysis included the potential option of using the mine's railroads for community transport and for cargo) and areas with high suitability for various crops.
- *Forest plantations.* The forest plantation scenarios mapped areas of high and medium suitability for three multipurpose tree species that are native to the region and could provide income for the local population as well as stabilize soils and enhance water retention. A recommendation for plantations of mesquite is linked to the proposal to introduce a zero-grazing, corral-based system for goat raising.
- *Livestock analysis.* The livestock scenario mapped current numbers of goats (estimated at 1 million) and areas suitable for the cultivation of trees that could serve as goat fodder among other uses. The large number of free-roaming goats has left large areas of Upper Guajira suffering from desert conditions, with denuded land and high levels of soil erosion.
- *Fishery and mariculture.* Spatial analysis mapped offshore areas of high yield for artisanal fishing and the main zones for industrial tuna and shrimp fishing, based on existing fishing activity. The planning team recommended a full analysis of the productivity of marine resources and carrying capacity to ensure sustainability as well as initiatives focused on improving the current fishing value chain, such as managing the cold chain and expanding the market.
- *Tourism and ecotourism.* The tourism scenarios considered issues of accessibility, biodiversity protection (especially in the region's national parks and bird conservation areas), current tourism nodes, and culturally significant areas. Analysis and subsequent planning focused on connecting the remote

and spectacular Upper Guajira area with existing tourism attractions, particularly the national parks and areas of high biodiversity through five distinct tourism corridors.

- *Mining infrastructure.* Areas related to the mining operation were mapped, as was railroad infrastructure connecting the mine with the port in Puerto Bolivar. While the use of the mining infrastructure for other purposes will require national government review and approval, the planning team recommends conducting a prefeasibility study on the potential for shared use of mining infrastructure (comprising railroads, airports, administrative, and residential infrastructure). This infrastructure could be of great support to the department's development, offering multimodal uses for sectors such as fishing, agriculture, energy, forestry plantations, tourism, and transportation.
- *Oil and gas.* Spatial analyses mapped current and potential future exploitation areas for oil and gas (La Guajira is the major gas-producing area of Colombia, providing more than 70 percent of national demand) as well as the main artisanal fishing areas, to identify potential incompatibilities or conflicts between these activities (problems are already emerging). Similarly, analysis showed how oil and gas development would need to take account of high-potential tourism areas in coastal and marine zones.
- *Renewable energy.* A combination of agricultural, tourism, and renewable energy potential revealed areas where wind and solar parks could be developed without affecting these other green growth sectors. These areas, with high potential for renewable energy and low potential for other development opportunities, may not have been considered in current plans for wind and solar farm initiatives due to their isolation and lack of well-maintained physical infrastructure, constraints that are addressed in the spatial analyses relating to accessibility and roads.
- *Conservation.* The conservation scenario looked not only at the need to conserve existing protected areas and consider nationally recognized environmental priority areas as no-go zones for future development but also at the potential for generating income through employment in the green economy (with crops such as vanilla, with tourism and job creation in new proposed protected areas and existing national parks, and so forth).
- *Restoration.* The analyses focused on water conservation and landscape restoration. Seventeen locations were identified for water basin restoration projects to improve water availability and to support other economic sectors such as tourism, agriculture, and fishing. The landscape restoration scenario was closely linked to the recommendation to reverse the destruction caused by free-ranging goats, in order to transform arid and desert areas into productive ecosystems that support the local economy's diversification.
- *Physical infrastructure.* The spatial analyses revealed priority areas for upgrading or constructing roads to improve the weak accessibility of large areas of La Guajira and to support the considerable tourism development opportunities. Analysis also generated recommendations for developing five cabotage ports in different points in the peninsula to improve maritime connectivity between local communities, enable more local procurement from currently isolated suppliers, and open new markets for local businesses. The planning team also suggested consideration of opening the mine's own airports and seaports for wider development purposes (passengers, fisheries, and cargo transportation).

More details are provided in the following sections on recommendations for promoting high-impact green growth in La Guajira.

Agricultural development

The suitability analyses of 16 different crops covered some that are already being grown in the department and others that are new to the area but being cultivated under similar conditions elsewhere. Separate models were produced to show suitability for both rainfed and irrigated cultivation systems. By combining this spatial analysis with the economic analysis for each crop, the planning team was able to identify the potential economic value for the total area of land suitable for each crop. Additionally, the spatial analyses included identification of areas suitable for the cultivation of a number of different crops (see map 3.2). These multicrop areas represent agricultural hotspots where favorable agroclimatic conditions can best accommodate a range of crops. Knowing the location of these hotspots is important for planning potential initiatives such as agroprocessing centers, cooperative production schemes,

MAP 3.2

Multicrop analysis (without irrigation)

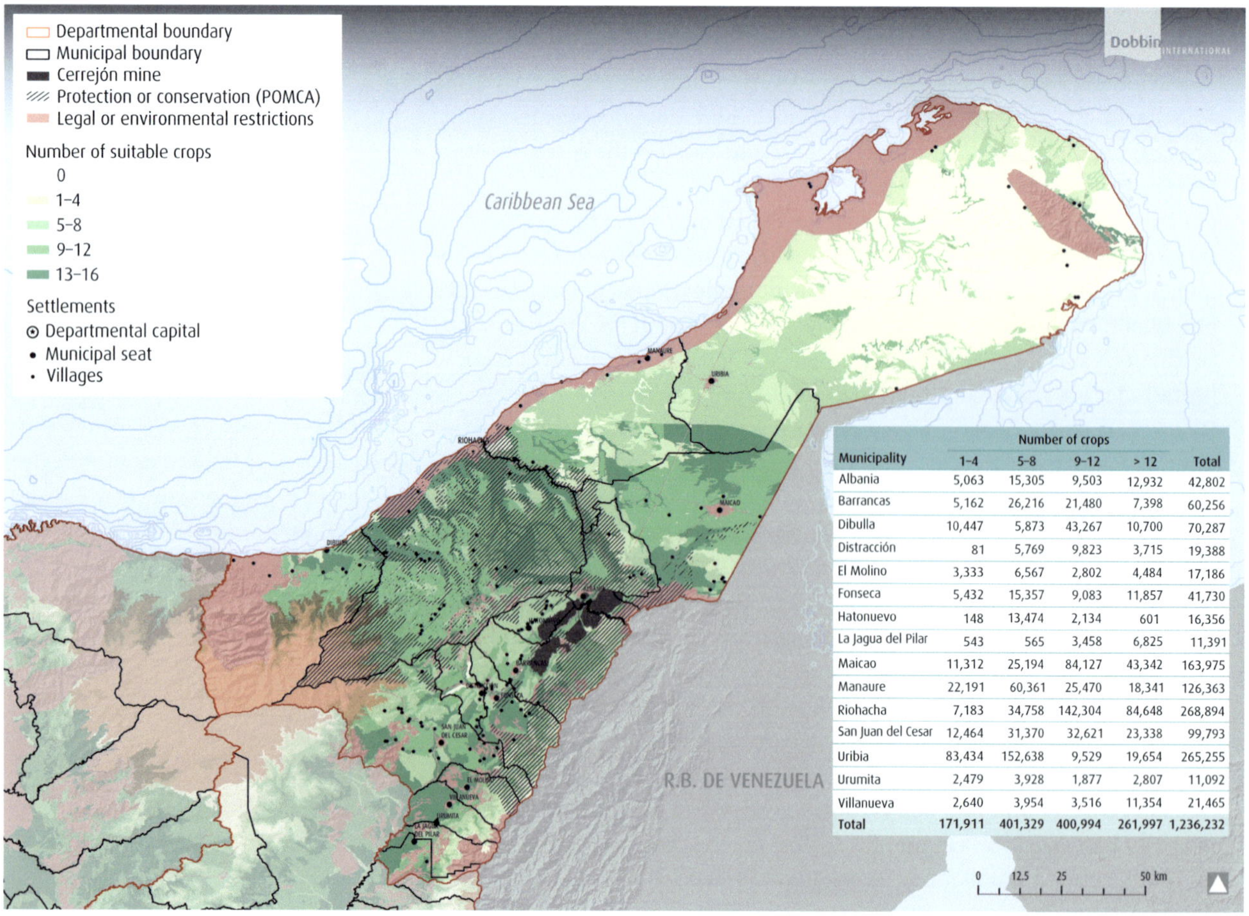

Municipality	Number of crops 1–4	5–8	9–12	> 12	Total
Albania	5,063	15,305	9,503	12,932	42,802
Barrancas	5,162	26,216	21,480	7,398	60,256
Dibulla	10,447	5,873	43,267	10,700	70,287
Distracción	81	5,769	9,823	3,715	19,388
El Molino	3,333	6,567	2,802	4,484	17,186
Fonseca	5,432	15,357	9,083	11,857	41,730
Hatonuevo	148	13,474	2,134	601	16,356
La Jagua del Pilar	543	565	3,458	6,825	11,391
Maicao	11,312	25,194	84,127	43,342	163,975
Manaure	22,191	60,361	25,470	18,341	126,363
Riohacha	7,183	34,758	142,304	84,648	268,894
San Juan del Cesar	12,464	31,370	32,621	23,338	99,793
Uribia	83,434	152,638	9,529	19,654	265,255
Urumita	2,479	3,928	1,877	2,807	11,092
Villanueva	2,640	3,954	3,516	11,354	21,465
Total	**171,911**	**401,329**	**400,994**	**261,997**	**1,236,232**

Source: Dobbin International 2020.

Note: POMCA = Planes de Ordenación y Manejo de Cuencas Hidrográficas. The table shows the number of high and medium suitability crops measured in hectares.

and irrigation systems. In addition to these production-related analyses, the planning team identified an urgent need to strengthen the agricultural value chains to create added value for local products and take advantage of the privileged geographical location of the department for potential exports to Aruba, Bonaire, and Curaçao.

Forest plantations

The analysis of commercial forestry opportunities examined potential for three types of plantations: trupillo (mesquite—a small leguminous tree), ollita de mono ("monkey nut," a nut-bearing tree, *Lecythis ollaria*), and teak (a hardwood). While areas suitable for teak plantations are limited to the southern part of La Guajira, monkey nut suitability extends farther north, and the nuts of this tree offer important commercial pharmaceutical and cosmetic uses thanks to their high content of oil and selenium. Extensive areas of the department (over 1 million hectares) are suitable for mesquite plantations (see map 3.3). This multipurpose tree is used for timber as well as for nutritional and medicinal uses by the Wayuu and, importantly, as fodder (see livestock analysis in the following section).

MAP 3.3

Mesquite (trupillo) suitability (without irrigation)

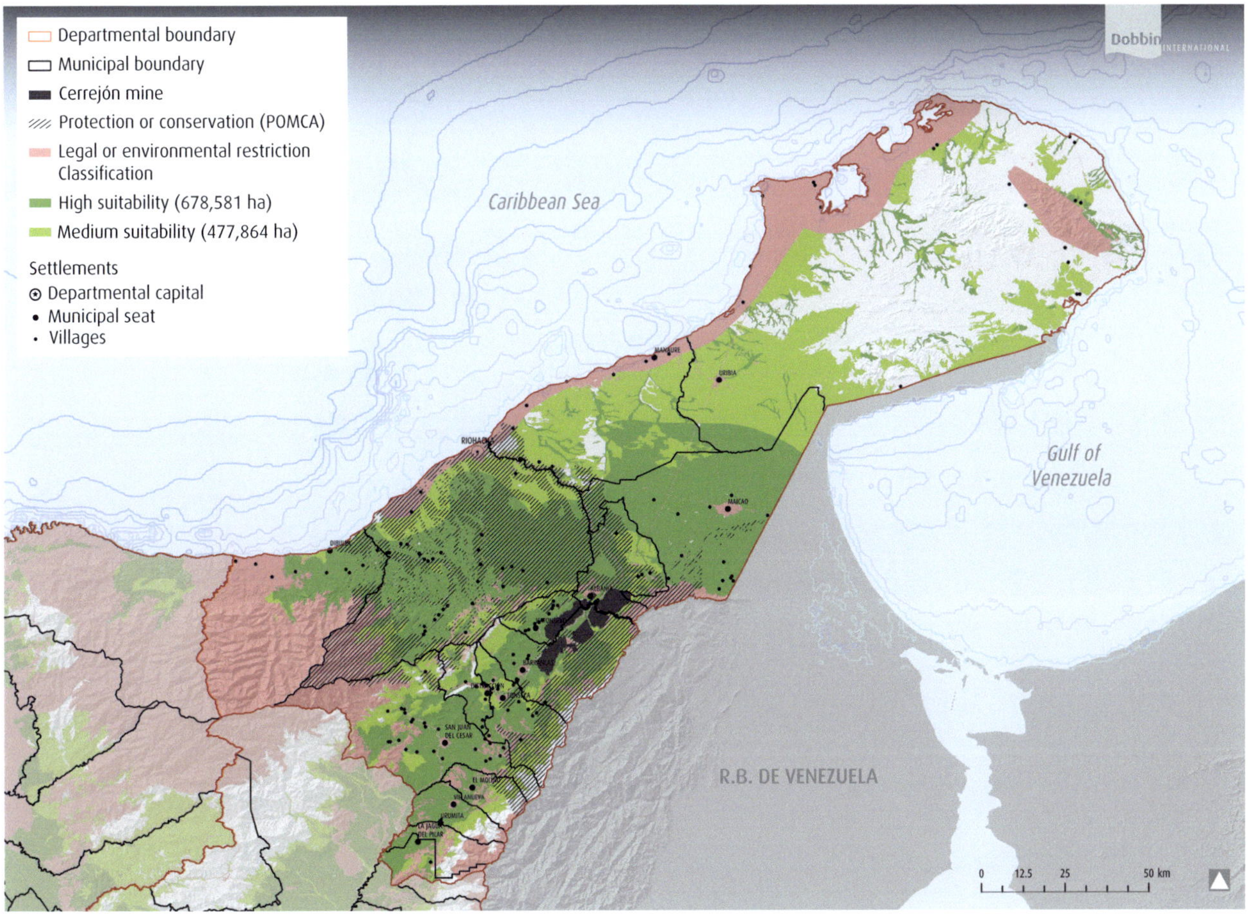

Source: Dobbin International 2020.
Note: ha = hectares; POMCA = Planes de Ordenación y Manejo de Cuencas Hidrográficas.

Livestock production

The livestock production analysis focused on goat rearing, which presents important opportunities—and challenges—for green growth in La Guajira. Goats have a strong economic and cultural importance for the indigenous Wayuu population, as symbols of wealth, as easily liquidated assets, and as sources of meat. According to the Instituto Colombiano Agropecuario, there are an estimated 1.5 million goats and sheep in La Guajira (approximately 59 percent of the total herd in Colombia (ICA 2020). This large number of free-roaming goats and sheep presents considerable environmental challenges, as evidenced by the denuded landscapes and widespread erosion seen in the northern section of the department. In contrast, fenced-off areas, such as around the coal-exporting port, show how natural vegetation can survive the harsh conditions if goats and sheep are excluded. The spatial analyses enabled the identification of a potential solution that respects both local culture and the environment—to switch from a free-roaming to a zero-grazing, corral-based system, which would increase the profitability of goat and sheep production while protecting and enhancing the vulnerable landscapes. Map 3.4 illustrates the potential for cultivating mesquite (a small leguminous tree) and prickly pear cactus

MAP 3.4

Goat production scenario

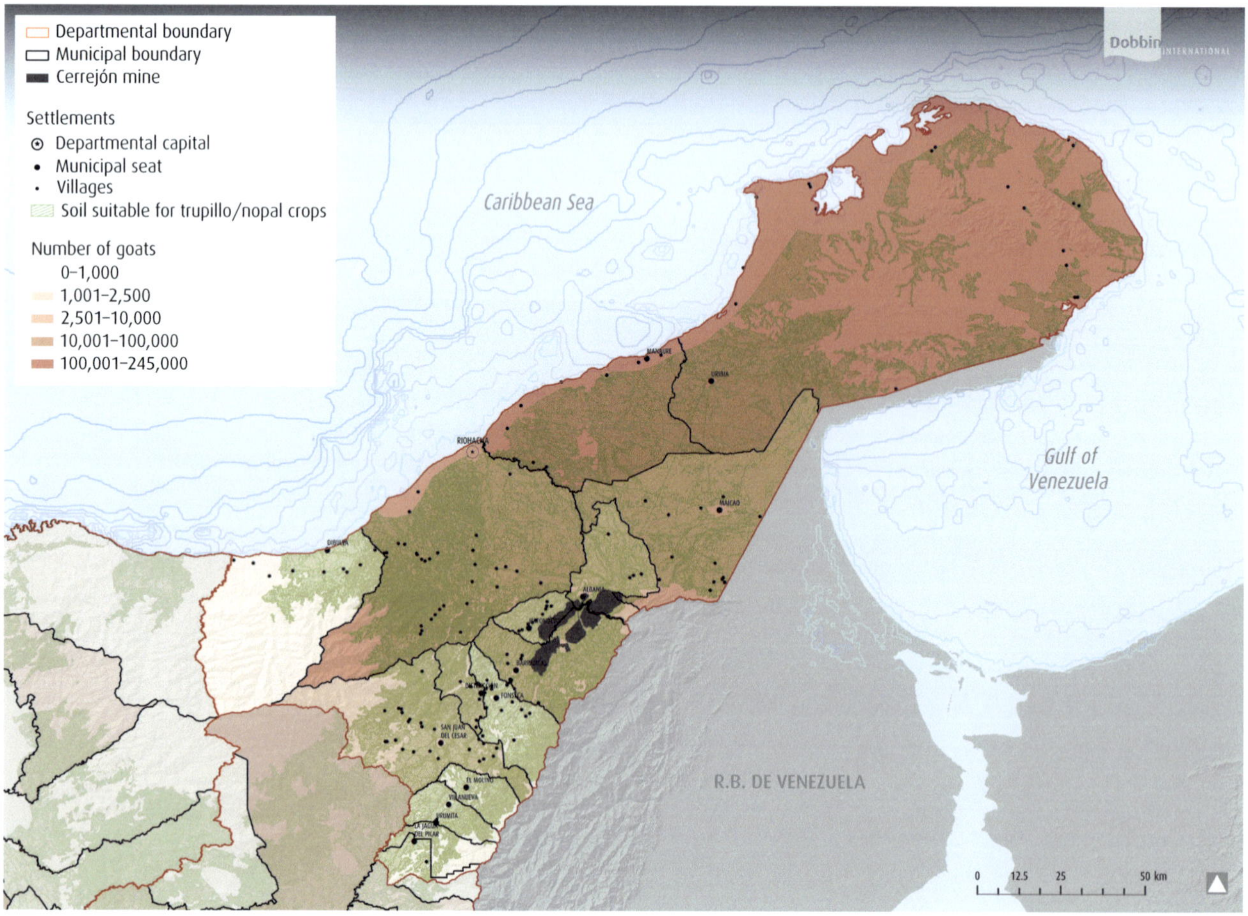

Source: Dobbin International 2020.

(a succulent)—two native species—in areas with high densities of goats and sheep, for use as goat fodder and for revegetation for soil conservation and water management.

Tourism and ecotourism

The analysis of tourism potential revealed strong opportunities for an enhanced and sustainable tourism sector in the department, enabling increased visitor levels from the current 30,000 visitors per year up to 200,000 visitors per year if infrastructure investments are made and if the priority projects identified in the analysis are implemented by 2040. From the spatial analysis, the planning team proposed five thematic tourism corridors, each connecting some of the department's unique tourism assets. These corridors cover: (1) adventure tourism, (2) ecotourism and adventure tourism, (3) cultural tourism, (4) ethnotourism, and (5) ecotourism and mining tourism (see map 3.5).

Renewable energy

La Guajira has exceptionally good potential for both wind and solar power, with strong winds and high levels of radiation. The spatial planning work took as its

MAP 3.5

Tourism and accessibility scenario

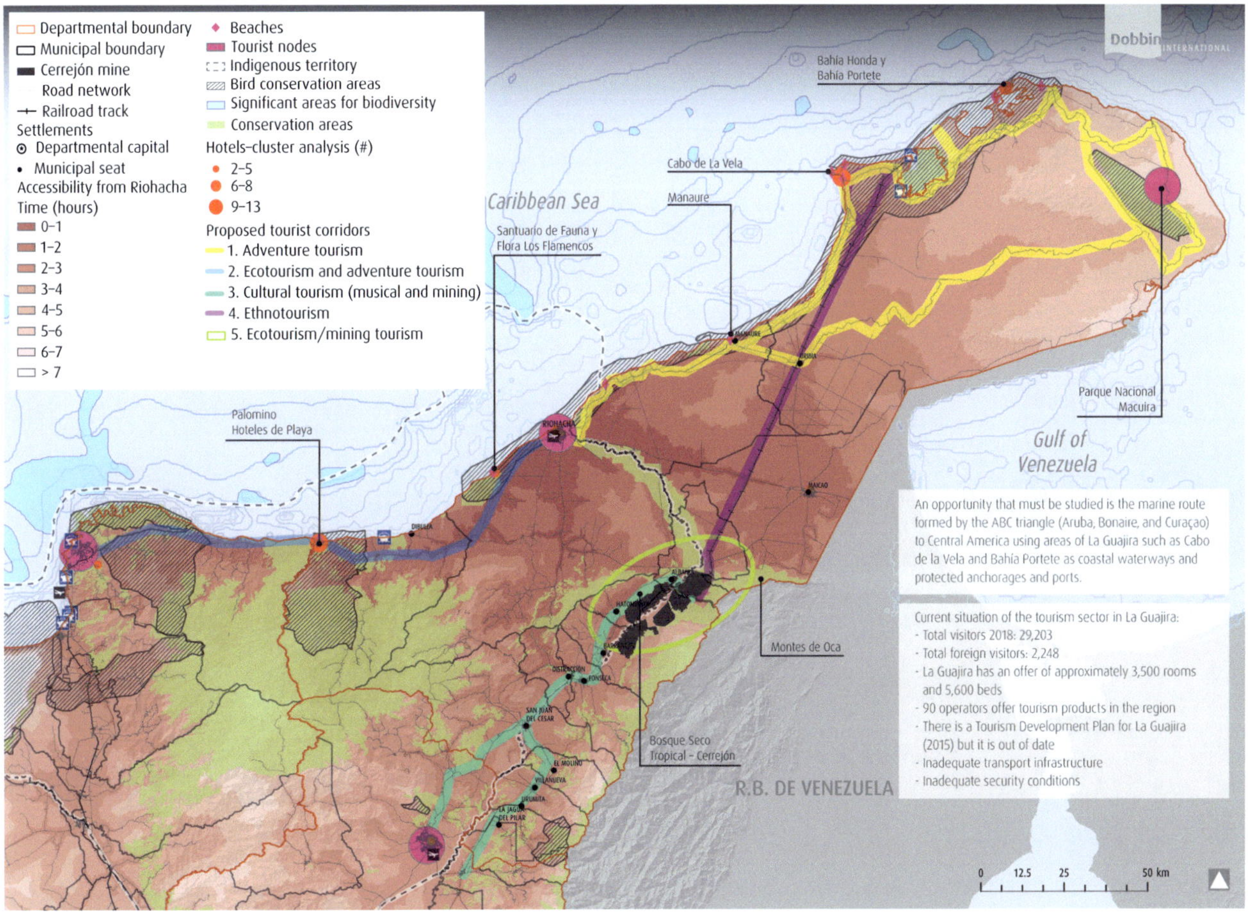

Source: Dobbin International 2020.

starting point that the development of these renewable energy sources should not benefit only large companies and that profitable yet financially accessible alternatives need to be developed for communities in the area to benefit from these resources. Close to 70 renewable energy projects are being approved or have been approved in La Guajira. However, there is an almost complete lack of small-scale solar projects in the area to expand Wayuu communities' access to electricity.

The analyses identified two large areas where wind and solar parks could be developed without negatively affecting other sectors such as tourism and agriculture (see map 3.6), while also identifying areas of potential conflict between renewable energy infrastructure and other sectors (mainly on the northern coast, where several wind farm projects have been proposed to the government). Developing the two most suitable areas for wind and/or solar energy would require upgrading road and port infrastructure—investments that would also support tourism, fishing, social services, agriculture, and so forth.

In addition, the planning highlighted a promising new technology, already being piloted in the northern desert of La Guajira, that uses solar energy to produce water (see box 3.3).

MAP 3.6

Renewable energy, agriculture, and tourism scenario

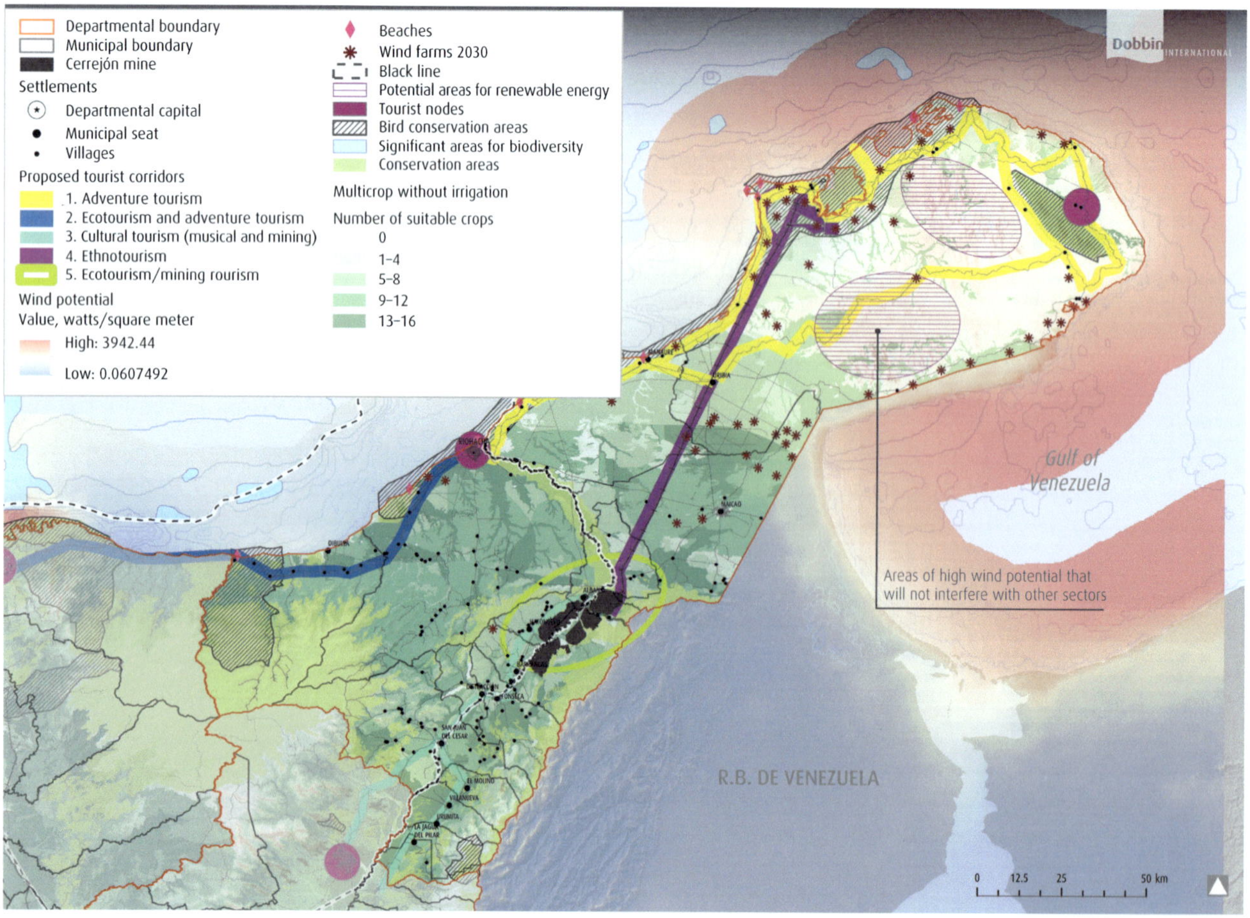

Source: Dobbin International 2020.

BOX 3.3

A new technology pilot in La Guajira: Using solar energy to produce water

A new technology, developed by Zero Mass Water and trademarked as hydropanels, produces clean, mineralized water from specially designed solar panels. Hydropanels can be a cost-effective source of drinking water for commercial applications (at worksites, community centers, schools, hotels, and tourism destinations) and residential applications. The panels produce water through a four-step process: (1) solar energy powers the off-grid panels, (2) fans draw in ambient air and push it through a water-absorbing material that traps water vapor from the air, (3) the water vapor is extracted and passively condenses into liquid that is collected in the reservoir, and (4) the water is ozonated and minerals are added to remove impurities and improve taste.

Hydropanels have been installed in some of the most arid deserts in the world. Two sets of panels have recently been installed in the community of Bahia Hondita on the northern coast of La Guajira, as a partnership between Zero Mass Water and Conservation International–Colombia.

Source: SOURCE n.d.

CLIMATE CONNECTIONS AND OTHER LANDSCAPE-ECOSYSTEM LINKS AMONG SCENARIOS

This section provides a narrative of some of the connections and links among scenarios. Further quantitative assessments of a number of these links using economic analysis tools are in the section "Supplementary Economic Analysis of Selected Climate Connections and Other Links" of chapter 4.

Each scenario described in the preceding subsections represents a set of potential interventions within a traditional economic sector or planning area. Connections among these scenarios, or to external factors, can present opportunities to realize synergies: instances where complementary processes or feedback reinforce activities in other sectors. Identifying such feedback and synergies relies on multiple disciplines working together at an analytical and planning level, as well as at a local administrative and institutional level. Support at a high policy level also helps.

By way of example, a number of themes illustrate how these synergies arise and how they can be addressed. Notably, lessons can be drawn from evaluating some mainstream development issues: (1) *climate change* connections, (2) effective *afforestation* as a multisector activity, (3) developing the so-called *blue economy*, and (4) improved *disaster risk management* and planning. These issues can be transparently and comprehensively addressed by the spatial planning process.

Climate change connections in the La Guajira planning area can be appreciated in the context of Colombia's nationally determined contribution (NDC) under the Paris Agreement (Colombia 2020). The country's NDC helps to mitigate climate change—through reducing greenhouse gas (GHG) emissions—while also adapting to the impacts of climate change. The existence of the NDC provides a strong policy basis for considering the climate change connections within and among scenarios. Examples of climate connections reflected in the La Guajira planning include the following:

- *Land suitability.* Analyses included simulation of soil conditions and suitability for agriculture (and forestry) under climate change scenarios that potentially reflect changes in water availability, temperature, soil quality, and pest incidence. Analyses of which areas are suitable for various crops are informed by such climate forecasts.
- *Renewable energy.* GHG emission reductions are implicit in transitioning to renewable energy through the development of forest plantations, promotion of community composting, or protection of natural ecosystems that fix carbon.
- *Physical infrastructure.* Adaptation opportunities that promote sustainable urban development in coastal habitats arise from investments in infrastructure meant to reduce damage from hazards such as wind and flooding.

Afforestation and avoided deforestation are complementary processes that have far-reaching consequences. Both reduce GHG emissions, but afforestation has cobenefits of landscape management in rehabilitating overgrazed lands (from livestock) and in providing expanded tourism experiences as wildlife reenters restored landscapes. Various ecosystem services (nutrient retention, water catchment integrity, and protection from winds) also benefit from extended forest cover. Local communities can obtain additional subsistence or cash value from nontimber forest products (NTFPs) such as pharmaceuticals, foodstuffs, and plant fibers; such values are sustainable and directly benefit local populations. Again, a policy commitment helps. In September 2019, Colombia hosted a workshop—"NTFPs: Prosperity through Our Wealth of Biodiversity"—led by the Global Green Growth Institute. At that workshop, the "Ministry of Environment and the National Planning Department spoke to the attendees about the regulatory framework for the use of NTFPs, the regulations associated with the use of forest by-products, and of how a Bioeconomy fits into the framework of the Green Growth Policy and the National Development Plan 2018–2022 for Colombia" (GGGI 2019).

The blue economy involves activities reliant on the goods and services provided by ocean resources (see Thiele et al. 2020). In a sustainable ocean economy, economic activities are in balance with the long-term capacity of ocean ecosystems to support these activities and remain resilient and healthy. Blue economy assets encompass both living and nonliving resources as well as ecosystems and ecosystem processes. They extend far beyond the fisheries sector, capturing a broad range of potential services: offshore mining, marine protected areas, space for wind farms, and cooling functions for arrays of data servers. The spatial planning approach can identify links that enhance ocean services and maintain this capital. Examples of blue economy connections reflected in the La Guajira planning include the following:

- *Urban infrastructure planning and recycling.* The reuse and recycling of plastics has become a more pressing issue as nations attempt to address the urgent problem of persistent plastic pollutants and wastes in the ocean environment. Some mining companies[1] have been instrumental in promoting plastics recovery during metal recycling operations, and infrastructure and business opportunities can be located and established strategically to improve the cost-effectiveness of shared assets.
- *Tourism planning.* The spatial development of tourism sites can be coordinated with other sectors to avoid location-related conflicts (for example,

fishery landing sites), reduce beachfront impacts in erosion-prone areas (through appropriate infrastructure), and allow access to high-value protected areas sustainably (for example, Bahía Portete-Kaurrele National Natural Park, Los Flamencos Fauna and Flora Sanctuary, and La Macuira National Natural Park) while sharing appropriately located road, sewage treatment, and other common infrastructure.

Hazard reduction and risk management are key to climate adaptation and particularly suited to the peninsular nature of La Guajira, which gives it a relatively large ratio of coastline to land, similar to that of a large island; it is very much a coastal department. Properly planned interventions will save lives as coastal populations continue to grow. Economic growth accompanied by higher incomes will also increase the values of coastal property and physical assets. The protection of lives, assets, and livelihoods is therefore another strong impetus for considering the links among sectors. Rangel-Buitrago and Anfuso (2009) estimate that 68.3 percent of the La Guajira coastline can be classified as very high or high vulnerability. Spatial planning allows us to identify ecosystems and areas that can perform joint functions: an intact mangrove ecosystem will absorb storm wind energy while also sequestering carbon, filtering municipal sewage, and providing a nursery for nearshore fisheries. The dune systems in La Guajira, when mapped, identify important protective buffers and are often treated as no-go areas for infrastructure development. Flood vulnerability mapping through the use of digital elevation models will inform urban planners regarding the design of public infrastructure. This can include drainage systems or—as was done in this case study—the siting of soccer fields to be used for temporary water retention in the event of floods.

Once again, an existing policy and institutional framework for operationalizing such interventions helps. Colombia stands out for its many successes in disaster risk reduction, which are implemented by the National Unit for Disaster Risk Management.[2] It was the first country to align its national development plan with the UN Sustainable Development Goals and the Sendai Framework. The Sendai Framework—a 2015 UN document arising from international meetings in Japan associated with risk management—explicitly integrates disaster risk reduction and action on climate change as conditions for resilient growth.

MAIN FINDINGS OF THE SPATIAL ANALYSES

Following the completion of all spatial analyses, the planning team identified seven key ways to capitalize on La Guajira's green growth potential as a foundation for the proposed vision, strategy, and action plan:

1. *Improve water availability*. While La Guajira is known for its water scarcity, some areas in the upper and middle regions of the department were shown to have considerable groundwater resources and seasonal surface water that are not being well managed. The analysis concluded that, with the right investments, water availability can be significantly improved.

2. *Restore the landscape for productive uses*. For hundreds of years, the free grazing of goats and sheep has brought with it massive land degradation in the upper and middle regions of La Guajira, and the loss of natural vegetation has

greatly reduced the landscape's capacity to retain water when it rains, which in turn has exacerbated soil erosion. Switching to a corral-based system of sheep and goat rearing would restore the landscape and increase the value of these animal products in the value chain.

3. *Promote tourism development across all of La Guajira.* La Guajira is renowned locally, nationally, and internationally for offering unique tourism experiences in remote areas. The analyses revealed the department's potential to expand in specialized markets such as bird watching, star gazing, and ethnic participation activities associated with the Wayuu culture. Removing key constraints to tourism development, by improving connectivity (Wi-Fi and cellular) and infrastructure (roads, ports, landing strips, and airports), would also support sectors such as renewable energy, agriculture, fishing, and transportation of goods and people, as well as enhance access to health and education facilities and banking and government services.

4. *Develop coastal and marine resources sustainably.* A lack of reliable scientific information on the department's coastal and marine resources limits decision-making. Initial analysis suggested strong potential for mariculture (algae), coastal and marine tourism, small recreational craft in the bay and the lagoon system of Upper Guajira, and possibly a solid marine transportation system through a series of cabotage ports. The analysis pointed to the need for a fish stock assessment to establish the current condition of the marine ecosystems and identify the carrying capacity for sustainable use.

5. *Farm alternative agricultural crops and high-value forest plantations.* The agriculture and forestry suitability models revealed innovative opportunities in La Guajira that offer potential for local farmers and established commercial farmers. Analyses considered a range of alternative crops, including the opportunity to use prickly pear, ollita de mono (monkey nut), and trupillo (mesquite) in Upper Guajira as feed for goats to reduce desertification and improve the quality of the environment, enhance water availability, and produce goat meat. The analysis also highlighted the urgent need to give added value to local products and take advantage of the privileged geographical location of the department for potential exports to Aruba, Bonaire, and Curaçao.

6. *Include Wayuu and local communities in socioeconomic development planning.* La Guajira is a multicultural department, with most of its territory belonging to indigenous communities. The analyses clarified the need to consult with these communities regarding any upcoming investments or initiatives and highlighted how to integrate Wayuu communities' participation and insights in the development of potential opportunities for employment generation and sustainable development.

7. *Reimagine and use Cerrejón's infrastructure for other purposes.* Given the planned closure of the Cerrejón mine by 2034, it is important to consider potential reuse options for the current mining infrastructure, including the airports, railroads, port of Puerto Bolivar, administrative offices, mine pits, and compensation areas. The analyses uncovered opportunities to support the export of local goods via the port, transport tourists using the railroad, create water reservoirs in the pits, and establish a national park in the compensation area, a dry tropical forest, that would connect the Sierra Nevada de

Santa Marta with the Serranía del Perijá. It would be necessary to first conduct detailed prefeasibility studies that review and assess all the issues associated with reimagining other uses of Cerrejón's infrastructure over the next 14 years and beyond.

NOTES

1. In 2008, Anglo American established joint ventures in Europe to facilitate plastic separation from automotive and other waste streams (see Holland 2008).
2. For more on the unit's activities, see its website, Unidad Nacional para la Gestión del Riesgo de Desastres, http://portal.gestiondelriesgo.gov.co/.

REFERENCES

Colombia. 2020. First Nationally Determined Contributions, Updated Submission. December 29, 2020. NDC Registry, UNFCC. https://www4.unfccc.int/sites/NDCStaging/pages/Party.aspx?party=COL.

Dobbin International. 2007. *Mozambique: Spatial Development Strategy for Palma District, Mocimboa da Praia District, Mossuril District, and Nacala Porto District.* A series of four reports prepared for the Ministry for the Coordination of Environmental Affairs (MICOA) funded by the World Bank. Herndon, VA: Dobbin International.

Dobbin International. 2010. *Southern Tanzania and Northern Mozambique: Spatial Development Planning Project—Perspectives on Regional Development.* Report prepared for the Aga Khan Development Network (AKDN), Chantilly, France. Herndon, VA: Dobbin International.

Dobbin International. 2013a. *Mozambique: Agro-Forestry Village Strategic Planning Project for Muembe District, Lichinga District, Sanga District, Chimbonila District, Mecuburi District, Ribaue District, Namarroi District, Ile District, Gorongosa District, Muanza District, Manica District, and Sussundenga District.* A series of reports prepared for the US Department of Agriculture and TechnoServe Mozambique. Herndon, VA: Dobbin International.

Dobbin International. 2013b. *Mozambique: Rio Tinto Coal—Regional Development Strategy Linking People, Places, and Potential—Tete-Macuse Corridor (Zambezi) Linking Zambezia, Sofala, Manica, and Tete Provinces.* Report prepared for Rio Tinto Mozambique. Herndon, VA: Dobbin International.

Dobbin International. 2013c. *Mozambique: Anadarko LNG—Igniting the Dream—Strategic Spatial Planning Project—How Dynamic Stability Can Create Prosperity for Cabo Delgado Province: Detailed Spatial Plans for Cabo Delgado Province, Palma District, and Pemba Town.* Report prepared for Anadarko Petroleum Corporation. Herndon, VA: Dobbin International.

Dobbin International. 2015. *Strategic Spatial Development Planning for the Mozambique Systematic Country Diagnostic (SCD).* Report prepared for the World Bank Group, Mozambique Country Office, July 2. Herndon, VA: Dobbin International.

Dobbin International. 2015–18. *Limpopo Provincial Strategy for Resilient Sustainable Development, Linking People, Places, Potential TM: South Africa, Limpopo Province, Mogalakwena Municipality, Thabazimbi Municipality, Musina Municipality, and Blouberg Municipality.* A series of 12 reports prepared for Anglo American, Anglo American Platinum, and DeBeers Group of Companies. Herndon, VA: Dobbin International.

Dobbin International. 2020. *Strategy for Sustainable and Resilient Development of La Guajira, Colombia.* Report prepared for Cerrejón mine. Herndon, VA: Dobbin International.

GGGI (Global Green Growth Institute). 2019. "Non-Timber Forest Products (NTFPs): The Prosperity of Meta through Its Richness in Biodiversity." News release, September 18, 2019. https://gggi.org/non-timber-forest-products-ntfps-the-prosperity-of-meta-through-its-richness-in-biodiversity/.

Holland, C. 2008. "Anglo-American JV Boosts Plastic Recycling." *Embedded,* January 4, 2008. https://www.embedded.com/anglo-american-jv-boosts-plastics-recycling/ Accessed October 2020.

ICA. 2020. *Censo Pecuario año 2020*. Bogotá: Instituto Colombiano Agropecuario. https://www.ica.gov.co/areas/pecuaria/servicios/epidemiologia-veterinaria/censos-2016/censo-2018.aspx.

Rangel-Buitrago, N., and G. Anfuso. 2009. "Assessment of Coastal Vulnerability in La Guajira Peninsula, Colombian Caribbean Sea." Special issue, *Journal of Coastal Research* 56 (2009): 792–96. http://www.jstor.org/stable/25737687.

SOURCE. n.d. "Perfect Drinking Water Created from Sunlight and Air." Scottsdale, AZ: SOURCE. https://www.source.co/.

Thiele, T., G. Alleng, A. Biermann, E. Corwin, S. Crooks, P. Fieldhouse, D. Herr, N. Matthews, N. Roth, A. Shrivastava, M. von Unger, and J. Zeitlberger. 2020. *Towards Sustainable Blue Infrastructure Finance: The Need, Opportunity and Means to Integrate Nature Based Solutions into Coastal Resilience Planning and Investments—Key Messages*. Gland, Switzerland: International Union for Conservation of Nature.

US Geological Survey, Richard Stockton College of New Jersey Coastal Research Center, Dobbin International, and The Futures Group. 2006. *Monograph on a Study of the Future Impact of Minerals, Hydrology, and Ecology on Integrated Regional Economic Development in the Anosy Region, Madagascar*. Report submitted to the Projet de Gouvernance des Ressources Minerales (PGRM), Madagascar, and to the World Bank. Herndon, VA: United States Geological Survey.

World Bank. 2006. *A Case Study in Dynamic Mineral Resources Management, Anosy Region, Madagascar*. Washington, DC: World Bank.

World Bank. 2016. *Republic of Mozambique—Systematic Country Diagnostic*. Report No. 103507-MZ, June 2016. Washington, DC: World Bank.

4 Development of a Strategic Plan for La Guajira

INTRODUCTION

Phase 3 of the planning work centered on a strategic spatial development plan for La Guajira, including economic analysis of alternative futures and the preparation of a "project bank" of prioritized initiatives.

This phase built on the spatial analyses and discussions of the earlier phases and continued the collaboration with key stakeholder groups to build a shared vision for La Guajira Department—to transform it over a 20-year time frame from an area heavily dependent on coal mining to one with a diversified and resilient green economy that attracts high-value investments while managing social and environmental challenges.

IDENTIFICATION OF DISTRICT PLANNING ZONES

Critical to this phase of strategic planning was the identification of seven distinct planning zones in the department, based on interpretation of recent satellite imagery and the earlier spatial analyses (see map 4.1). The relatively homogeneous biophysical conditions in each zone mean that each has a specific set of characteristics, opportunities, and constraints. Detailed maps were prepared for each zone and sets of specific opportunities outlined. These detailed maps can inform appropriate policies, projects, and actions to unlock the potential of each area.

The seven proposed planning units of La Guajira are as follows:

1. *Upper green Guajira:* An isolated area with mountain ranges, including cloud forest
2. *Upper desert Guajira and coastal zone:* Rolling hills and salt flats, green only in the rainy season and heavily degraded by the overgrazing of goats

MAP 4.1

Seven planning zones identified for La Guajira

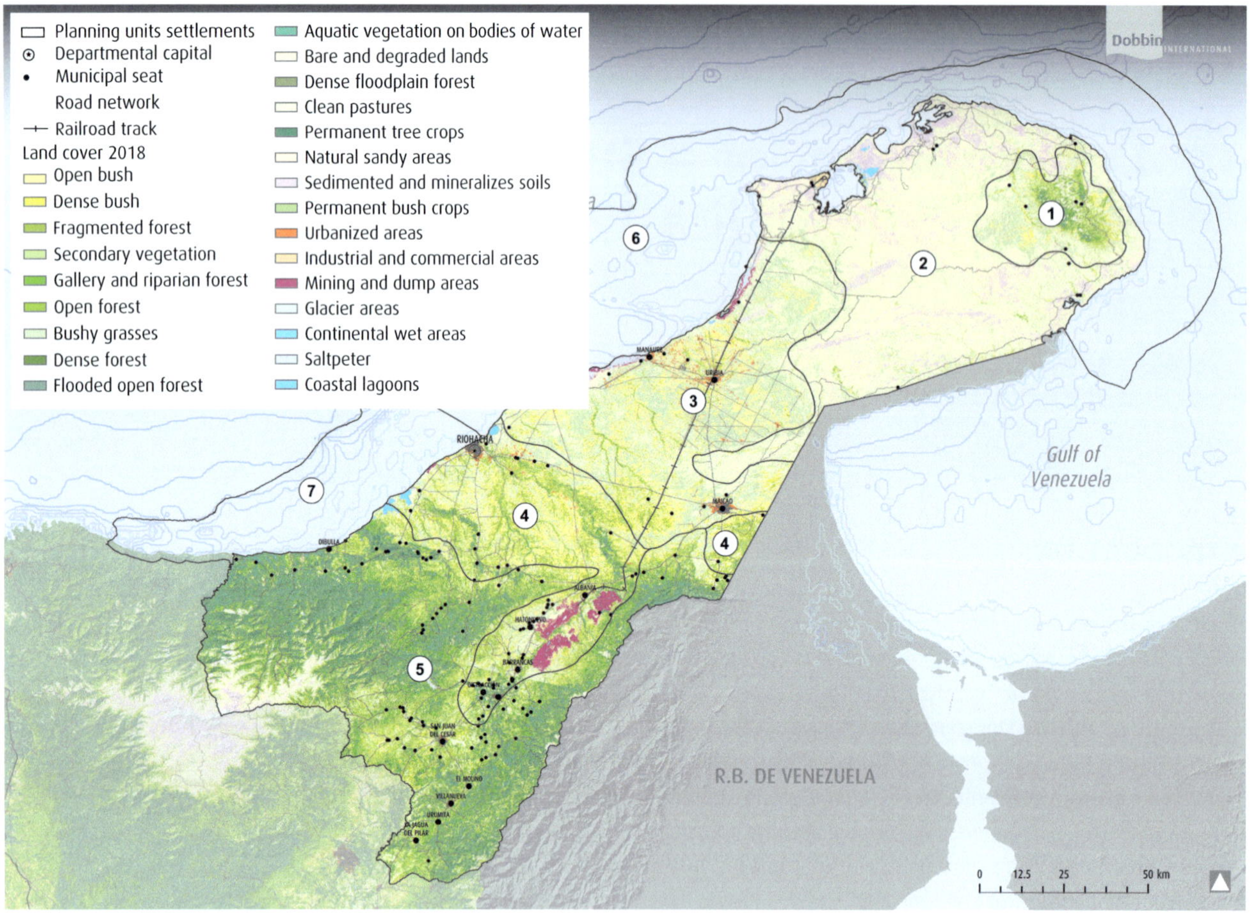

Source: Dobbin International 2020.

3. *Mid-desert Guajira and coastal zone:* Relatively flat area with less water availability than in the north but rich in marine habitats and bird biodiversity
4. *Lower Guajira and coastal zone:* A fertile area with relatively good water availability and possibility of irrigation from the Rancheria River, with high levels of ethnic diversity (Wayuu, Afro-Colombian, and Venezuelan migrants)
5. *Lower mountainous Guajira and coastal zone:* A steep and mountainous area in the foothills of the Sierra Nevada, with good water availability and fertile soils but some slopes too steep for farming
6. *Upper marine Guajira:* A maritime zone with soft sediment, coral, and seagrass meadows
7. *Lower marine Guajira:* A more brackish zone with hard sediment, strong currents, high-energy waves, and mangrove forests

Extrapolating from this more granular analysis, an overall strategic plan was developed for the department as a whole (see figure 4.1 and map 4.2). While recognizing that the current economic drivers will continue to be important in the short to medium term, six new drivers and five new support drivers of green growth were identified: agriculture, forest plantations, fisheries, tourism, beekeeping, innovative livestock management, conservation, restoration, urban development, social infrastructure, and physical infrastructure. These represent new opportunities to gradually replace the mining revenue on which the department currently depends. The strategic plan also incorporates five new "support drivers," critical underpinnings of the economic growth opportunities. These support drivers consist of conservation and restoration initiatives as well as urban development and infrastructure development programs.

Box 4.1 describes how an application of the spatial development planning approach in South Africa has led to the establishment of an investment platform to support the implementation of collaborative initiatives.

FIGURE 4.1

Strategic plan for La Guajira

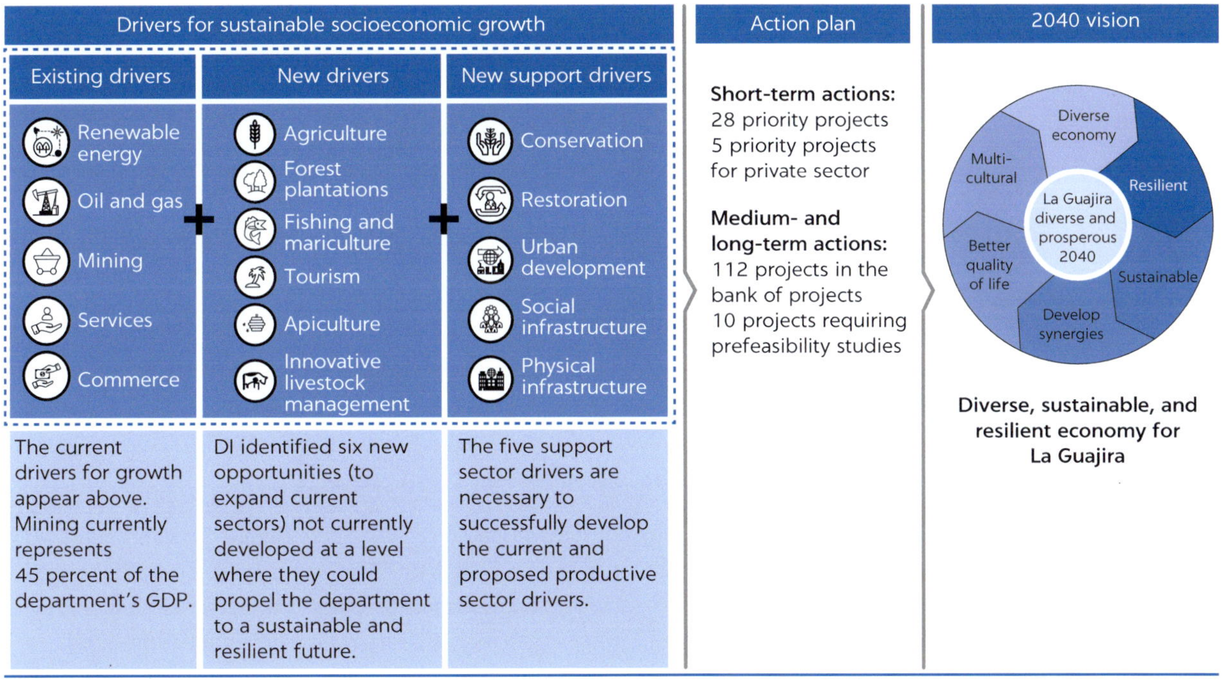

Source: Dobbin International 2020.
Note: DI = Dobbin International; GDP = gross domestic product.

MAP 4.2

Mapped vision for La Guajira in 2040

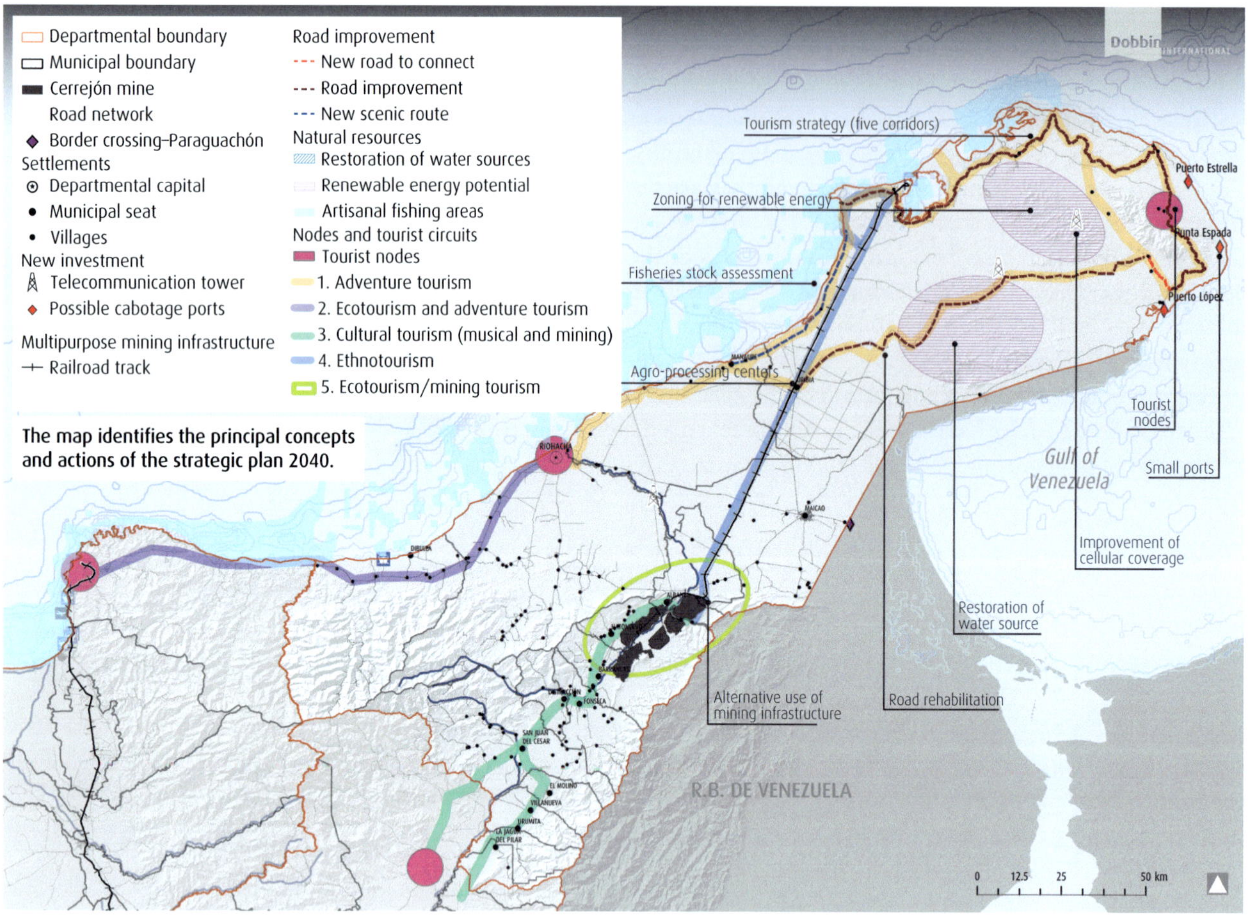

Source: Dobbin International 2020.

BOX 4.1

South Africa: A strategic plan leading to an investment platform

In 2015, Anglo American commissioned Dobbin International to undertake strategic spatial development plans for South Africa's Limpopo Province and four of its municipalities (Mogalakwena, Thabazimbi, Blouberg, and Musina) where the company operates. The objective of the planning was to identify constraints and opportunities to unlock the province's and municipalities' potential for poverty reduction and economic growth, focusing on building resilience to the downturn in the mining sector by developing a vision, a strategic framework, and examples of investment opportunities (including pilot projects).

The strategic spatial development planning work ran for three years (2015–17) and involved a multidisciplinary team including spatial planners, sustainability experts, spatial analysts, and environment and development economists. The planning process considered such issues as water availability, poverty distribution, and climate change and established key achievable targets for new green growth opportunities in areas suitable for smart agriculture, forest plantations, conservation, restoration, tourism, and ecotourism.

Dobbin International proposed a set of specific recommendations from the planning, including initiatives to take advantage of the potential synergies

continued

Box 4.1, *continued*

between the mining operation and local development, including, for example: production and agroprocessing of guar bean, which can be used in platinum processing (historically, the mine site was importing 1,000 tons of guar bean annually from India for this purpose) and similarly for Moringa, a multiuse crop that can be processed into excellent-quality biofuel that can be used in mining equipment and vehicles and has numerous other applications.

Recommendations were also made for enhancing the management of protected areas and developing better links between these areas and tourism circuits to benefit Kruger National Park.

More broadly, the planning work reimagined the existing provincial growth strategy, which focuses primarily on urban growth nodes and the obvious major urban and highway corridor connecting Limpopo to Pretoria and Johannesburg. This corridor leaves out 65 percent of the province's population and offers little potential for agriculture or forest plantations, as it is built on the dry sandy ridgeline. Instead, the planning and modeling focused on the poorest regions of the province, where strong potential was revealed for agricultural development, forestry, agroprocessing, game farming, biofuel, and other opportunities. The strategic framework and project proposals developed during the planning work later formed the basis for Anglo American's collaborative regional development program in Limpopo, involving the private sector, the government, nongovernmental organizations, and research partners. It also served as the foundation for the establishment of collaborative investment projects in Limpopo Province and municipalities and is now referred to by Anglo American as the "impact catalyst."

Sources: Dobbin International 2015–18; Dobbin International and ThirdWay Africa Partners 2016.

BUILDING A PROJECT BANK

The strategic plan and the opportunities identified for each planning zone were then taken forward to develop a list of proposed projects for implementation by the public sector, the private sector (including Cerrejón), other actors, or through collaborative efforts. A "project bank," in the form of a spreadsheet, was prepared for some 112 projects, outlining the proposed initiatives and categorizing each as (1) an economic stimulus investment or (2) a support investment. The support investments relate to natural resource management, urban development, or infrastructure development initiatives, which—while not directly driving economic outcomes—are essential for underpinning sustainable development and green growth. The database tool enables users to apply different filters and prioritization criteria to select projects of interest for follow-up. It also shows points of synergy between each support investment and the economic stimulus investments.

From this set of 112 projects, 28 were identified as top priority, based on eight specific criteria and qualitative analyses derived from workshops, field assessments, discussions with experts, economic analysis, and professional judgment and experience. The eight selection criteria are as follows:

1. *Easy wins*: Projects that can be implemented in the near future for the benefit of communities located in the mine's direct area of influence (5 of the 15 municipalities in La Guajira), by Cerrejón or other actors and without the need for partnerships or special implementation mechanisms to be developed

2. *Game changers*: High-impact projects that unlock the potential for one or several economic sectors in a step-change manner
3. *Income and employment support*: Projects that facilitate new value chains at the local, regional, national, or international level, generating significant boosts for local incomes and employment
4. *First key step*: Projects that enable the collection of robust and reliable scientific information required to start or structure other innovative interventions that have been included in state development plans (municipal, departmental, regional, or national) but not yet realized
5. *Activators of development drivers*: Projects that activate one or more of the development drivers defined in the strategic plan during the strategic spatial development planning
6. *Key environmental actions*: Projects that respond to the main environmental challenges identified through the planning process
7. *Cost-benefit analysis*: Projects with a benefit-to-cost ratio greater than unity
8. *Alternative use of mining infrastructure*: Projects that are aligned with the mine's closure plan and enable existing mining infrastructure to be used for development purposes

The 28 projects, all of which meet at least one of the above criteria, are listed in appendix C. A project profile was prepared for each of these 28 initiatives, including information on the proposed location, the main activities foreseen, type of projects (private, public-private partnerships, prefeasibility studies), priorities taken from research and stakeholder analysis of issues, constraints and opportunities, and the likely level of investment needed. The strategic plan envisaged coordinated implementation of these priority projects in order to take advantage of the cross-sectoral synergies that will be needed for the full development potential of the department to be realized.

Economic analyses and projections

Of the 28 prioritized projects, 13 high-impact projects were chosen for an in-depth economic analysis of their economic viability and socioeconomic impact. The analysis revealed high potential for significant improvements in economic growth, employment, income generation, and poverty reduction. For example, the proposed investments in ports and roads were estimated to provide more than 8,500 jobs during the life of these projects, while the proposed agricultural initiatives were estimated to account for the bulk (75 percent) of potential employment generation benefits, which amount to nearly 50,000 jobs by 2040. This increased employment was estimated to generate a 65 percent increase in per capita income in the department. On this basis, assuming the 13 priority projects are implemented (entailing a US$660 million investment) and the Cerrejón mine closes in 2034, the department's gross domestic product (GDP) was estimated to grow, reaching US$5.2 billion in the same time frame, based on 2018 prices. By comparison, the current annual GDP in La Guajira is approximately US$3.5 billion, and its recently approved development plan for 2020–24 envisages investing only 5.85 percent of the total budget envelope of US$460 million in economic diversification and strategic infrastructure projects.[1]

FIGURE 4.2
Potential GDP growth for La Guajira (mine closure)

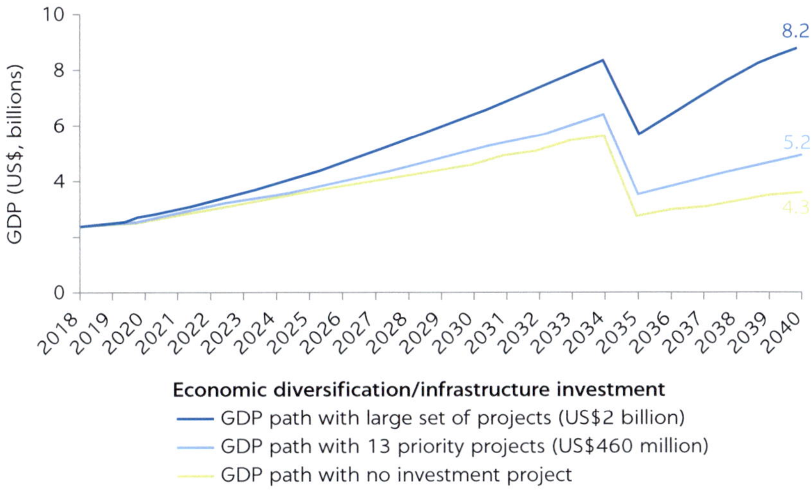

Source: Dobbin International 2020.

Implementation of a fuller set of projects, an investment totaling nearly US$2 billion, would enable the department's GDP to reach US$8.2 billion by 2040, more than offsetting the overall economic impact of mine closure.[2] This increased investment would replace mining revenue with a diversified economy built on increased agriculture, tourism, infrastructure, forest plantations, commerce, and potentially fishing and mariculture (see figure 4.2).

SUPPLEMENTARY ECONOMIC ANALYSIS OF SELECTED CLIMATE CONNECTIONS AND OTHER LINKS

Spatial planning software allows the identification of land suitability to a fine level of detail. A 30 by 30 meter pixel can be extrapolated to larger areas (hectare or square kilometer) when combined with neighboring pixels. When supplemented with standard microeconomic analysis models for agriculture, forestry, biodiversity conservation, or other landscapes, it is possible to generate potential economic values of different scenarios. In the discipline of environmental economics, the general literature also provides estimates of various environmental and ecosystem functions, which do not necessarily flow through formal markets as other goods and services would.

A large body of work has also informed a process of *benefit transfer*, which takes starting values from carefully studied primary sites and transfers those to comparable sites or landscapes. When a valid set of starting values has been curated, these can be applied to broad landscapes to provide economic values to different land uses, or to indicate values at risk if the landscapes become degraded. Dobbin International has applied such valuation techniques in different contexts to provide guidance to policy initiatives and sustainability issues. In particular, such valuations can signal potential for revenue capture when appropriate economic instruments (user fees, taxes, tradable permits, and so forth) can be introduced to monetize otherwise untraded commodities.[3] This section investigates the calculation of values associated with some of the links introduced in "Climate Connections and Other Landscape-Ecosystem Links among

Scenarios" in chapter 3. In particular, methods are applied to consider values associated with the blue economy and carbon emissions reduction in forestry and agriculture; a representative analysis of protected areas in Colombia is also presented, which can be extrapolated to one or more of the protected areas in the study area.[4]

Valuation of the blue economy

This process remains methodologically complicated, but global values would attribute a potential value equivalent to approximately US$1 million annually for every kilometer of productive coastline. This extends well beyond just fishery values and includes value-added processing as well as other productive values of coastal processes. The coastline in La Guajira is characterized by an active, productive fishery, featuring approximately 80 fishery landing sites or ports used by 130 fishing associations along 600 kilometers of coastline. A direct transfer of the valuation basis suggests that a potential value of US$600 million annually is realistic for the study area. To place this in perspective, Colombia's *national* exports of tilapia fish alone (from aquaculture) have exceeded US$50 million in recent years. Given that the GDP of La Guajira is approximately US$3.5 billion per year, fishery and other ocean-based values represent a potentially large future contributor to economic production. As with many ocean assets, the limited information base on fisheries cannot inform what levels of exploitation are sustainable for wild resources. The sustainability of trends toward shore-based aquaculture—while positive in terms of export values and local food production—is also difficult to judge: this can have pollution impacts or risk introducing invasive species to local ecosystems. For this reason, valuations in this realm should be regarded only as indicative of potential in comparison to other values (such as GDP) that have robust accounting behind them.

Valuation of carbon emission reduction in forestry and agriculture

Emission reductions arising from landscape changes can be estimated with established methodologies and models using Intergovernmental Panel on Climate Change (IPCC) conventions. Those reported here rely on methods established through the United Nations Framework Convention on Climate Change and the Ex-Ante Carbon-balance tool of the Food and Agriculture Organization, applying tier 1 IPCC emission factors. These are expressed in net terms for a land-use change or adoption of a new technology, with all emission changes then translated to an equivalent carbon dioxide (CO_2) forcing. Methane, for example, has more impact as a greenhouse gas (GHG) than does CO_2, hence methane emissions from organic decay would have a greater detrimental impact than CO_2 emissions. All impacts are eventually reduced to their equivalence in CO_2, and a standard unit of emission reduction is therefore designated as a *ton of carbon dioxide equivalent* (tCO_2e). A price of carbon can be applied based on market conditions for tradable permits, or on avoided cost methodologies. A recent World Bank review and survey—*State and Trends of Carbon Pricing 2019*—suggested that the minimal price range needed by 2020 consistent with achieving Paris Agreement targets was in the range of US$40–US$80 per tCO_2e (World Bank Group 2019).[5] This case study uses a value of US$60 per tCO_2e for illustrative purposes.

As shown in appendix C, a number of priority projects were identified during the spatial planning exercise in La Guajira. Those in forestry and agriculture were chosen across different parts of the study area, based on the suitability of growing conditions. In some of these specific projects, an analysis of water and carbon values was undertaken directly. For example, the reforestation of 150 hectares in Rondas de los Ríos generates modest joint benefits for water conservation and climate change mitigation over its 30-year life. The project assessments also show that a forest plantation on 2,000 hectares generates US$19 million annually in direct income, and that new crops on 51,000 hectares generate US$120 million in export benefits. These serve as useful comparisons. As a whole, however, the landscape potential is considerably larger. For illustrative purposes, based on land suitability assessments conducted for this project, we can consider landscape potential to be approximately 1 million hectares for each of agriculture and forestry. Typical GHG emission reductions for such landscapes are estimated to be greater than 10 tCO_2e per hectare and greater than 30 tCO_2e per hectare, respectively; this assumes some incorporation of agroforestry in an agricultural setting. This yields a total annual mitigation of >40 million tCO_2e, with an imputed value of US$2.4 billion per year.

Valuation of protected areas in La Guajira

The spatial planning work in this case study identified a number of potential protected area and conservation initiatives in the tourism sector. An area that is world renowned for its flamingos—the Los Flamencos Fauna and Flora Sanctuary—covers a gazetted area of 7,000 hectares, although the estuary is larger. In comparison, the Bahía Portete–Kaurrele National Natural Park is 14,080 hectares in extent, but similarly has a much larger buffer area. The Macuira National Natural Park, located near Nazareth in the High Guajira, has an area of 25,000 hectares. The Sierra Nevada de Santa Marta National Natural Park has 383,000 hectares, of which 157,450 (41 percent) are located in the La Guajira department. Some of the natural areas in La Guajira are already in protected status, while some would benefit from being gazetted in a higher class of protection.

Although significant work has been done globally on the valuation of protected areas, it remains one of the most elusive for using benefit transfer methods because many of the values are specific to circumstances in a given country and are not easily transferred among countries, even if sites are similar. Partially this is because of inconsistent treatment of buffer areas. Also, however, an approach to park system valuation in a country or subregion tends to be more useful than valuation of a specific protected area. Much of the literature therefore attributes values that fall in a wide range and depend very much on local conditions. Early work by the World Bank and International Union for Conservation of Nature (Pagiola, von Ritter, and Bishop 2004) shows data and examples for which values are typically US$100–US$1,000 per hectare per year to an order of magnitude estimate, and these remain relevant to any benefit transfer exercise. Of that, about two-thirds can be attributed to direct uses such as timber extraction, nontimber forest product gathering, or recreation, with the balance attributable to conservation functions and watershed protection. Also, approximately half is captured locally through traditional use of natural areas and their ecosystem services. Analysis of the Colombian Andes (Bello et al. 2013), by contrast, attributes values in excess of US$165,000 per hectare per year (in 2011 prices) to the conservation of montane landscape. (The authors, however, warn that their estimates are from a limited sample size and may not apply other montane sites or other ecosystems.) The wide valuation range provided by the literature makes the use of benefit transfer in these circumstances inadvisable. More extensive surveys across ecosystems and scales in the country are advisable.

NOTES

1. For a detailed analysis of the regional government's investment strategy, see Colombia (2020).
2. This fuller set of projects would ideally be chosen from among the 28 priority projects and would reflect the most current priorities at the time of selection.
3. For examples in the region, see Huber, Ruitenbeek, and Serôa da Motta (1998) on Latin America and Sánchez-Triana et al. (2020) on the Yucatán.
4. This section was written by Jack Ruitenbeek. Some results rely on a curated and validated in-house information database of global valuation results maintained by the author.
5. Actual prices in the survey were in the range of US$1–US$127 per tCO_2e with an unweighted median of US$10 per tCO_2e.

REFERENCES

Bello, C., C. A. Ruiz-Agudelo, and L. F. Madriñan-Valderama. 2013. "Aproximación a la valoración de algunos de los servicios ecosistémico de los andes colombianos, a partir de una transferencia de benéficos por meta-análisis." *Capital Natural de Colombia* 4. Bogotá: Conservación Internacional Colombia. https://docs.google.com/file/d/0B5we0mcGmul5TjlRMVZMRFl0TTg/edit. An English version may be found at http://www.conservation.org.co/media/R6.capital_natural_No4_english_22012014%20F.pdf.

Colombia. 2020. *Plan Departamental de Desarrollo de la Guajira: Unidos por el Cambio 2020–2023*. Riohacha, La Guajira, Colombia: Equipo de Gobierno Departamental. https://laguajira.gov.co/web/attachments/article/6157/Paln%20de%20Desarrollo_compressed.pdf.

Dobbin International. 2015–18. *Limpopo Provincial Strategy for Resilient Sustainable Development, Linking People, Places, Potential TM: South Africa, Limpopo Province, Mogalakwena Municipality, Thabazimbi Municipality, Musina Municipality, and Blouberg Municipality.* A series of 12 reports prepared for Anglo American, Anglo American Platinum, and DeBeers Group of Companies. Herndon, VA: Dobbin International.

Dobbin International and ThirdWay Africa Partners. 2016. "Changing Outcomes in Africa—The Pathway to Multi-Sector High-Impact Investment for Shared Prosperity." Concept note for the Senior Director of the World Bank's Agriculture Global Practice. Herndon, VA. Dobbin International.

Dobbin International. 2020. *Strategy for Sustainable and Resilient Development of La Guajira, Colombia.* Report prepared for Cerrejón mine. Herndon, VA: Dobbin International.

Huber, R., H. J. Ruitenbeek, and R. Serôa da Motta. 1998. "Market-Based Instruments for Environmental Policy Making in Latin America and the Caribbean: Lessons from Eleven Countries." Discussion Paper 381, World Bank, Washington, DC. http://documents.worldbank.org/curated/en/508741468224411187/pdf/multi-page.pdf. A Spanish version may be found at http://documents.worldbank.org/curated/en/294221468016840626/pdf/WDP38110SPANISH.pdf.

Pagiola, S., K. von Ritter, and J. Bishop. 2004. "Assessing the Economic Value of Ecosystem Conservation." World Bank Environment Department Paper 101 in collaboration with the Nature Conservancy and International Union for Conservation of Nature, World Bank, Washington, DC.

Sánchez-Triana, E., J. Ruitenbeek, S. Enriquez, and K. Siegmann. 2020. *Opportunities for Environmentally Healthy, Inclusive, and Resilient Growth in Mexico's Yucatán Peninsula.* International Development in Focus. Washington, DC: World Bank. https://openknowledge.worldbank.org/handle/10986/31724.

World Bank Group. 2019. *State and Trends of Carbon Pricing 2019.* Washington, DC: World Bank. https://openknowledge.worldbank.org/handle/10986/31755.

5 Planning for Green Growth: Key Insights and Lessons Learned

KEY INSIGHTS FROM THE GREEN GROWTH PLANNING IN LA GUAJIRA

Through its combination of expert analyses, stakeholder consultations, field assessments, and professional interpretation of spatial patterns and trends revealed by the use of satellite imagery and other maps, the strategic spatial development planning approach enables valuable insights for unlocking the potential of an area. The following are some of the insights gained through the work in La Guajira.

Important interlinkages for green growth potential. The analysis showed how different factors—positive and negative—intersect spatially, revealing new understandings of the potential for green growth. For example, the poorest area in the north of La Guajira is also the area with the highest level of land degradation and weakest accessibility; at the same time it is also the most promising area for wind and solar energy production and has strong potential for date palm plantations. In addition, while the northern area is highly water stressed and rivers here flow only in the rainy season, the spatial analysis showed that this area also includes zones of high lineament density (indicating groundwater recharge) and absorbent soils. With appropriate water-retention interventions (such as check dams and riparian buffer zones), the area has high agricultural potential.

Synergies for green growth. The planning sought to identify and exploit synergistic opportunities for green growth. For example, the rehabilitation of a road that traverses the northern area of the department would provide better access for the isolated communities there and better connections for a tourism circuit that takes in both the northern and southern coasts. Road rehabilitation would also open the areas proposed for solar and wind energy and for agriculture projects. These high-potential areas are currently difficult to access due to the bad condition of the road network. In another example, the installation of solar-powered hydropanels on the roofs of homes would provide shade and irrigation for garden crops as well as water and electricity for households.

Improved locations for green energy. The planning revealed that, while La Guajira offers strong potential for renewable energy, the numerous permit applications for wind and solar energy projects in the department under government review are all planned for suboptimal locations along the northern coast. Installing wind turbines in these areas would compromise the attractiveness of high-potential tourism zones and would also generate less energy than if they were located inland. The planning identified areas in Upper Guajira as the most suitable locations for wind farms, based on their more favorable wind conditions and the fact that installations here would not conflict with other land uses in this sparsely populated zone.

Climate-proofed production opportunities. By taking into account the best available climate change forecasts for the area from Instituto de Hidrología, Meteorología y Estudios Ambientales (the Colombian government climate agency) and building future climate change impacts into the agricultural and forestry suitability models, the planning team outlined agriculture and forestry production initiatives that can be sustained under anticipated harsher conditions (elevated temperatures and significantly reduced rainfall, particularly in the southern part of La Guajira).

Opportunities for strengthening existing nature-based livelihoods. The spatial analyses revealed surprisingly high potential for enhancing existing nature-based livelihoods, with relatively simple interventions. These include, for example, constructing an abattoir for producing goat meat commercially and establishing seedling nurseries to boost the production of native trees for goat fodder and for landscape restoration.

Opportunities for green urban development. The planning work considered the opportunities for green urban development. Potential interventions were identified for four towns in La Guajira. In Riohacha, for example, a flood-prone area was designated a "sponge park" as a part of a green infrastructure proposal: sports facilities (playing fields) could be quickly and temporarily converted when necessary into water storage areas to mitigate flooding.

Opportunities for infrastructure for green growth. The planning team identified the need for prefeasibility studies for developing shared use of the Cerrejón mine infrastructure (including rail, ports, and airports) for development purposes. The coal-exporting port, for example, could support the export of fish and fish products, and agricultural products as well as tourism development. Additionally, the road, small ports, and landing strips will open isolated areas for ecotourism, adventure tourism, agriculture, and renewable energy.

CHALLENGES FACED IN CONDUCTING THE PLANNING WORK

The planning work did not encounter any major technical or logistical difficulties. However, the COVID-19 pandemic did interrupt the process toward its end, as did worker strikes that halted operations and hindered communications with key mine personnel involved in the planning. Furthermore, despite repeated efforts, it was very difficult to connect with the relevant government bodies in La Guajira and Bogotá to the degree required for optimal outreach and stakeholder engagement. Greater collaboration will need to be pursued at a later stage.

FROM PLANS TO ACTION

The various applications of the planning approach always seek to consider how investments will be organized in each specific context. This can be challenging, given that the planning team is not generally involved in the follow-up stages.

In La Guajira, the main follow-up activities required to start implementing the strategic plan include the following:

- *Launch an internal and external communication strategy.* The immediate next step will be to present the strategic plan to Cerrejón management and then to key external actors, including local, department, regional, and national governments.
- *Consult with government, other potential partners, stakeholders, and investors.* An intensive engagement process will be required to reach groups not included in the earlier consultations. This will be important in order to build a common vision among different stakeholder groups, manage expectations, and start conversations around potential roles, responsibilities, and collaborations. See appendix D for a summary analysis of the main interests of some key stakeholder groups.
- *Integrate the strategic plan into government policies and strategies.* For long-term impact, the strategic plan will need to be integrated into public policies at the local, regional, and national levels. This includes policies on green growth and climate change (see box 1.1, chapter 1), coal mining, and labor market issues.
- *Undertake additional research.* The planning work identified specific areas where additional research is necessary (for example, on fisheries-related investments). These will need to be conducted prior to detailed planning.
- *Establish a structure to implement the strategic plan.* A critically important step will be the establishment of an independent organization or investment platform to steer and coordinate implementation of the plan and to assess and monitor progress. Detailed discussions will need to take place with public and private sector actors, including Cerrejón, about their role in the investment platform.
- *Integrate the strategic plan into the mine's long-term planning.* As with its integration with public policies, the strategic plan will need to be integrated with Cerrejón's planning measures, including its closure and postclosure planning.
- *Develop the prioritized initiatives.* The proposed prefeasibility studies and the 28 prioritized projects (see appendix C) will need to be developed through various partnerships (for example, involving government, the private sector, international organizations, and nongovernmental organizations), exploiting the cross-sectoral synergies that have been identified (see box 5.1).

The risks associated with the implementation stage depend largely on the extent to which these follow-up activities are successfully completed. In addition, unexpected consequences of external threats such as COVID-19 and worsening climate change conditions would bring further risks, as would a failure to synchronize the cross-sectoral development strategies embedded in the planning (see boxes 5.1 and 5.2).

BOX 5.1

A synchronized implementation to exploit cross-sectoral synergies

The 28 priority projects are intended to be implemented in a synchronized manner, in order to start them all at roughly the same time, rather than in a sequence, so that advantage can be taken of the synergies that have been built into the strategic plan. Without this synchronized multisectoral approach, the anticipated economic benefits will not be fully realized. For example, if the tourism development projects are initiated prior to the road rehabilitation investments in the north of La Guajira, the economic benefits will be much reduced, and the feasibility of the proposed wind energy projects in the same location will be compromised unless their timing is also coordinated with the upgrading of the roads.

To facilitate this coordinated implementation, the planning team developed a "synergy matrix" to show which projects rely on supporting investments in conservation, restoration, physical infrastructure, and urban development. This tool also helps to identify partnerships and joint work with local authorities and communities required for each project and identifies synergies among all the sectors.

BOX 5.2

Lessons in implementing strategic spatial development plans: Example from Madagascar

The follow-up to planning work in the Anosy Region of Madagascar (described in box 2.3, chapter 2) provides useful lessons on factors that can affect implementation.

The 20-year Regional Development Framework (RDF) action plan was implemented, in part, with significant positive outcomes, including the following:

- Construction of a multiuse port near Fort Dauphin (now also known as Tolagnaro) by Rio Tinto and the World Bank, now used for ilmenite shipments and small regional cruise ship landings
- The development of the Fort Dauphin/Tolagnaro urban gateway and growth pole (urban roads, lighting, hospital upgrades, market relocation, airport rehabilitation, and so forth) through the Integrated Growth Poles Project (IGPP) by the World Bank
- Rio Tinto's construction of an ilmenite mine that remains fully operational

However, the full potential of the region, identified in the RDF, was not realized, as key elements of the plan were not implemented. For example, the multiuse port was intended to be utilized for other value-added uses (such as agroprocessing and fish processing), but this has not materialized. And among the growth poles identified in the plan, only the urban growth pole was developed, leaving the rest of the region largely neglected.

The reasons for only partial implementation of the RDF include the following:

- Key stakeholders, leaders, and participants in the regional development planning process left the Anosy Region after the plan was completed (with some moving into high-level positions in government), and so much of the local knowledge and momentum behind the plan's implementation was lost.
- The region was overwhelmed by the IGPP and never was able to reorganize with the same initial momentum to implement the RDF. (For example, there was no creation of a viable investment platform to market the plan and attract private sector investors.)
- While the RDF was developed for the 38 communes of the Anosy Region, President Ravalomanana later extended the region to a total of 64 communes to take advantage of its economic growth. Subsequent to this expansion of the region, there was never a concerted planning effort to revise the plan to create a regional development strategy for all 64 communes.

continued

Box 5.2, *continued*

In addition, major changes to the collaborative decision-making mechanism, which had led the development of the RDF, negatively affected the follow-up. The democratically elected, nonpolitical, and community-led Committee for Regional Development, with over 300 members, was replaced by government-led district administrators' leadership. The new leadership lacked the sense of urgency that locally led community leaders (whose livelihoods depended on successful implementation of the plan) had brought to the planning.

Sources: Dobbin International and CRD de l'Anosy 2001–05; Landscapes/Paysages 2008.

The strategic spatial development planning approach has been successfully applied in different contexts. However, the planning approach is not infallible: it will be successful only if certain conditions are realized. These preconditions include a collaborative approach to the planning, a strong up-front commitment to follow through on implementation of the plans, and a planning team skilled in systems-based creative thinking that takes a multisectoral approach.

LESSONS LEARNED FROM APPLYING STRATEGIC SPATIAL DEVELOPMENT PLANNING

Drawing on the planning team's experience in using the strategic spatial development planning approach in various contexts, the green growth framework may be complemented in the following ways:

- Development of opportunities for multisectoral synergies based on natural resource potential
- Climate-proofed planning and conservative scenarios regarding environmentally sensitive areas
- Consideration of support drivers of economic development (that is, conservation and restoration) as foundational elements for growth, rather than (as is sometimes the case in other economic planning) as afterthoughts to be implemented "if there is money left over"
- Environmental and economic analyses integrated with spatial analysis, with a view to identifying opportunities for generating financially sustainable operations that also generate direct benefits to local populations
- Focus on catalyzing shared value from the presence of an industrial operation, such as a mine (for example, its infrastructure, local content needs, water management, and so forth)
- Identification of opportunities that leverage existing expertise within the mining community to address resource management issues elsewhere in the department (for example, plastics recycling in conjunction with metal recycling, and security expertise in parks management)
- Planning for a postclosure green economy and sustainable livelihoods from the earliest stage possible (based on agriculture, forestry, tourism, conservation, restoration, and so forth)
- Agility to deal with emerging issues—the plan is not heavily reliant on any one initiative and so can accommodate changes in, for example, the economic viability of a particular crop or access to a particular market

- Spatial planning to identify optimal land-use allocations, taking into account all sectors (as in this case, where potential for wind energy conflicted with tourism potential along the coast, as was currently planned, and spatial planning identified better locations for wind energy development).

CRITICAL SUCCESS FACTORS

Experience has shown that collaborative approaches involving mining companies working in partnership with other economic actors take time to develop and require dedicated personnel to ensure continued engagement with the other parties. In some cases, organizational changes in a mining company (for example, delays or disruptions to the mining project, or changes in leadership or ownership) have stalled or blocked implementation of strategic plans. The example from Madagascar outlined in box 5.2 illustrates the kinds of challenges involved.

Government support for, and participation in, strategic spatial development planning is essential for ensuring follow-up and alignment with public sector policies and strategies. In some cases, regional governments have been among the strongest supporters of the approach, viewing the process and the outputs as valuable bases for prioritizing the use of development resources. However, it can sometimes be challenging to persuade mining companies to open the planning process before they see what outcomes emerge and what commitments they want to make to the implementation of the strategic plan.

More broadly, governments can play an active role in facilitating and complementing the use of this kind of collaborative planning approach by, for example, undertaking the following:

- Initiating a strategic spatial development planning process within the context of national or regional development, green growth, or poverty alleviation strategies
- Coconvening or mandating a collaborative regional development planning approach with mining companies and other economic actors
- Establishing green growth strategies that incorporate collaborative planning approaches
- Encouraging cross-sectoral collaboration between relevant government bodies to facilitate stronger multisectoral development strategies

REFERENCES

Dobbin International and CRD (Comité Régional de Développement) de l'Anosy. 2001–05. *Anosy: Schéma de développement régional (SDR)—Rapport de la Phase 2: Diagnostics préliminaires, Rapport de la Phase 3: Collecte d'informations pertinentes, Rapport de la Phase 4: Analyses—Les Grandes Orientations pour le Développement de la Région, Rapport de la Phase 5: Synthesis—Schema de Developpement Regional (SDR) de l'Anosy.* A series of four reports prepared for the CRD de l'Anosy, Fort-Dauphin, Madagascar. Herndon, VA: Dobbin International.

Landscapes/Paysages. 2008. "Madagascar: Unlocking the Potential." Interview with James Dobbin in *Landscapes/Paysages Magazine* 10 (4). https://www.csla-aapc.ca/sites/csla-aapc.ca/files/Landscape%20Paysages/Fall2008_0.PDF.

6 Conclusions: Advancing Green Growth

The strategic spatial development planning approach offers a well-established and proven framework for designing green growth strategies at any level, from municipality to national and beyond. Used within an extractive context, the approach enables companies to have a demonstrative effect on catalyzing local development and to build a shared vision for an area in collaboration with other stakeholders and economic actors.

While recent applications of the approach have most often been commissioned by extractive companies, it is equally applicable in other contexts for national or regional development planning or, as seen in Mozambique, to support national-level diagnostics of development constraints and opportunities for framing future interventions.

No matter what the context, government support and participation are essential if the planning is to generate lasting benefits in terms of sustainable investments. National and regional governments can play critical roles in initiating, coconvening, or mandating the use of such collaborative planning approaches.

The planning approach aligns closely with the green growth framework and expands the framework beyond its primary focus on water management, renewable energy, and physical infrastructure to encompass a wider range of sectoral initiatives based on the conservation, rehabilitation, and management of natural resources. Used in the development of strategic plans, the approach takes a conservative perspective on the carrying capacity of an area's environmental resources, building climate change projections and no-go zones (including environmentally sensitive areas) into the suitability analyses. And the identification of economic opportunities focuses on ensuring that the natural resource base is managed sustainably for productive uses, with conservation and restoration seen as critical underpinnings of economic growth. Strategies for unlocking an area's potential are based on the synergies that can be gained from a coordinated set of nature-based initiatives (such as novel multiuse agricultural crops or trees, or enhancement of the area's tourism potential) and infrastructure investments (such as rehabilitation of roads or development of ports).

As with any planning approach, its contribution in each application relies on subsequent implementation of plans and projects. While implementation may be affected by many other factors (including, for example, the extent to which the different stakeholders involved share the same vision and commitment), the collaborative nature of strategic spatial development planning helps create the necessary conditions for buy-in and follow-up by the different actors involved. The mechanisms that have been created to implement plans developed by this approach include a regional multistakeholder committee with strong representation of local communities, and a partnership between the main economic actors to create an investment platform for coordinated implementation.

Given the successes seen in using this planning approach in different contexts, it offers strong potential for further adoption. Whether undertaken in development assistance programs, shared value initiatives, or public sector planning, the approach can help mainstream green growth at multiple levels.

APPENDIX A

Methodology: Four Phases of Dobbin International Spatial Planning Process

FIGURE A.1

Four phases of Dobbin International's spatial planning methodology and process

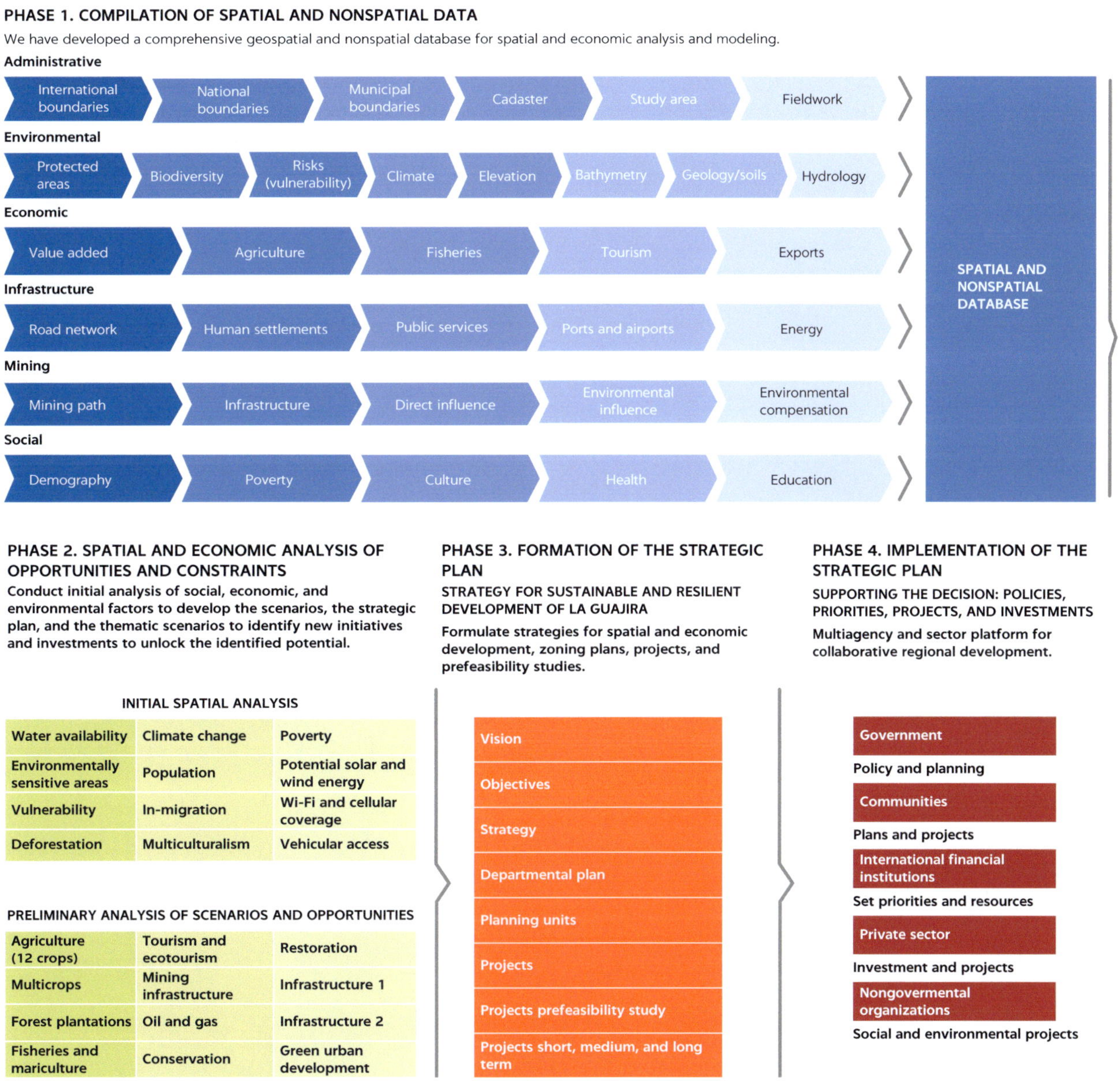

Sources: Dobbin 1976a, b.; Dobbin International 2020. © Dobbin International. Used with the permission of Dobbin International. Further permission required for reuse.

REFERENCES

Dobbin, James. 1976a. "Marine Park & Reserve Planning: Planning, Design, and Management of Marine Parks and Reserves." Thesis, Harvard University, Graduate School of Design, Department of Landscape Architecture, (Charles Harris, Chairman), Cambridge, MA.

Dobbin, James. 1976b. "Ocean Planning: Systematic Planning of Ocean Resources in the Exclusive Economic Zone." Paper, Massachusetts Institute of Technology, Legal Aspects of Ocean Resources Management, Course Number 15.966 (J.D. Nyhart, Associate Professor, Maritime Law), Cambridge, MA.

Dobbin International. 2020. Strategy for Sustainable and Resilient Development of La Guajira, Colombia. Report prepared for Cerrejón mine. Herndon, VA: Dobbin International.

APPENDIX B

Database Structure

TABLE B.1 **Database structure**

CATEGORY	SUBCATEGORY	DATA
Economic	Agriculture	Vocation and capacity, conflicts, productivity for the sector
	Fishing	Resource distribution, fishing techniques, productivity of the sector
	Mining	Wells, ducts, and exploration blocks
	Tourism	Tourist attractions, natural attractions, corridors, tourist clusters, beaches
	Productivity	Added value of Colombia's exports to Latin America and the rest of the world
Infrastructure	Physical accessibility	National, departmental and local roads, tolls, ports and airports, evaluation models
	Human settlements	Urban seat, populated centers
	Electric power	High-voltage lines, coverage
	Wind energy	Wind farms, projects
	Solar energy	Potential, parks, projects
	Water supply	Water salinity, reservoirs, water solutions
	Telecommunications	Infrastructure for connectivity, cellular networks, projects
Social	Culture	Indigenous reservations, culturally important areas, sacred sites
	Education	Schools
	Population	Population distribution, rancherias, communities, sectors
	Urban	Projects
	Health	Hospitals
	Socioeconomic	Multidimensional poverty, Gini
Administrative	Cadaster	Property division
	Political administrative boundaries	International, national, departmental, and municipal
	Fieldwork, WBS	Air, land, and maritime
Environmental	Protected areas	National, regional, local
	Coastal and maritime biodiversity	Maritime ecosystems, coastal environmental units, coral, coastal wetlands, mangroves, marine sea grass and pastures, turtle areas, preservation sites, beaches and coasts
	Ground biodiversity	Ground ecosystems, bird preservation areas, biosphere reserve, Ramsar wetlands
	Weather	Precipitation, radiation, temperature, climate change
	Ground coverage	Land use (2012–15), land coverage (2018)
	Geology	Land, faults, guidelines
	Hydrology	Drains, swamps, irrigation districts, earthen dikes, wetlands, basins, sandbanks, reservoirs
	Risks	Erosion, removal, hoods

continued

TABLE B.1, *continued*

CATEGORY	SUBCATEGORY	DATA
Agriculture	Parameters	Fertility, texture, Ph, drainage capacity, elevation
	Aptitude models	Evaluation with and without irrigation, multicrop models
	Restrictions	Environmental areas, physical infrastructure
Cerrejón	Environmental	Direct influence, indirect influence, compensation areas
	Railway line	Railway line, direct area of influence, environmental influence area, level crossings, port road
	Mine	Mining advancement, zoning, loan, property division, sections
	Protects	Protects, perturbation
	Resettlements	Original settlement, resettlement
Elevation	Topography	Elevation model, slopes, drainage models
	Level curves	Terrestrial, bathymetry

Source: Dobbin International 2020.

REFERENCE

Dobbin International. 2020. *Strategy for Sustainable and Resilient Development of La Guajira, Colombia*. Report prepared for Cerrejón mine. Herndon, VA: Dobbin International.

APPENDIX C

List of 28 Prioritized Projects

TABLE C.1 **List of 28 prioritized projects**

SOCIOECONOMIC AND ENVIRONMENTAL DRIVERS FOR SUSTAINABLE GROWTH	PROJECT NUMBER	DESCRIPTION OF THE PROJECT	SHORT, MEDIUM, OR LONG TERM
Agriculture	1.	Develop the value chain to cultivate vanilla in compensation areas for the Cerrejón mine	Short term
	2.	Implement a pilot watermelon project in the municipality of Albania	Short term
	3.	Develop a pilot beekeeping project in the compensation areas of the Cerrejón mine	Short term
	4.	Position La Guajira as an agricultural and exporting department	Medium and long terms
	5.	Develop 51,359 hectares of high-impact crops and export 8% of the yield (67,332 tons of agricultural projects with added value) to the Caribbean islands	Medium and long terms
	6.	Implement phases 2 and 3 of the irrigation district Rancheria River	Medium and long terms
Forest plantations	7.	Evaluate the timber value chain, develop 500 hectares of timber crops, and build a timber processing plant for export and local market production	Medium and long terms
Fisheries	8.	Develop jointly with Invemar a stock assessment and carrying capacity study for the coastal and marine zone of La Guajira	Medium and long terms
	9.	Perform a prefeasibility study to develop the mariculture potential along the coast of La Guajira	Medium and long terms
	10.	Build a fish processing and storage plant in La Guajira	Medium and long terms
Tourism	11.	Transform the Fauna and Flora Sanctuary in partnership with Parques Nacionales Naturales into a more attractive tourism destination	Short term
	12.	Develop Nazareth as an ecotourism hub in the tourism strategy	Medium and long terms
	13.	Promote a partnership with ProColombia, Ministry of Commerce, Industry, and Tourism to develop the five suggested tourism corridors	Medium and long terms
	14.	Work with Uribia to seek financing and revitalize Cabo de la Vela	Medium and long terms
Conservation	15.	Designate the suggested protected departmental areas and develop their management plans	Medium and long terms
	16.	Reforest the Macuira National Natural Park	Medium and long terms

continued

TABLE C.1, *continued*

SOCIOECONOMIC AND ENVIRONMENTAL DRIVERS FOR SUSTAINABLE GROWTH	PROJECT NUMBER	DESCRIPTION OF THE PROJECT	SHORT, MEDIUM, OR LONG TERM
Reforestation	17.	Reforest the perennial and seasonal river riparian areas and groundwater, WBS recharge areas	Medium and long terms
	18.	Develop a pilot project with the Bahia Portete or Media Luna communities to migrate to a goat and sheep corral system with prickly pear, trupillo, and moringa as feed	Short term
Physical infrastructure	19.	Reinforce or construct a cabotage port in Riohacha	Medium and long terms
	20.	Construct five cabotage ports in High Quanta	Medium and long terms
	21.	Expand the Riohacha Airport to an international standard airport (for goods and people)	Medium and long terms
	22.	Construct and rehabilitate the Cabo de la Vela, Nazareth road	Medium and long terms
	23.	Construct the 60-km coastal shoreline road from Manaure to Cabo de la Vela	Medium and long terms
	24.	Improve the internal roads of Nazareth	Medium and long terms
Mining—infrastructure of the Cerrejón mine (prefeasibility studies)	25.	Use Port Bolivar to export agricultural products, pending prefeasibility study	Medium and long terms
	26.	Use Cerrejón mine's railroad to transport tourists and agricultural products, pending prefeasibility study	Medium and long terms
	27.	Use the mine's airport and Puerto Bolivar for tourists, pending prefeasibility study	Medium and long terms
	28.	Design dry tropical forest compensation areas as a natural national park	Medium and long terms

Source: Dobbin International 2020.

REFERENCE

Dobbin International. 2020. *Strategy for Sustainable and Resilient Development of La Guajira, Colombia.* Report prepared for Cerrejón mine. Herndon, VA: Dobbin International.

APPENDIX D

Summary of Stakeholder Analyses

TABLE D.1 **Summary of stakeholder analyses**

STAKEHOLDER GROUP	INTERESTS
National government	Coal is currently the second-most-important export in the national economy, and Colombian coal production represents 8 percent of the global market. In 2019, Cerrejón provided the Colombian government with US$534 million in taxes and royalties, accounting for 23 percent of Colombia's total mining revenue. At the same time, the Colombian government has pursued a green growth strategy outlined in Colombia's 2018 Green Growth Strategy. The major challenge that the coal-mining sector faces involves planning the transition for regional economies that are highly dependent on coal mines. This is the case for departments like La Guajira and César, where communities' demand for adequate economic diversification planning has been rising. The national government is currently drafting specific policy guidelines for coal mining in Colombia; these would include continuous dialogue among stakeholders to determine the scale and ideal timetable for transitioning toward a more sustainable development model; the planning and monitoring of commitments, in a participatory manner, by all those involved; provisions for temporary support to workers and their families through social protection programs; and the deployment of active labor market policies that offer programs and incentives to encourage both new jobs and the transfer of skills among workers. The actions identified by the Ministry of Mines and Energy, from a strategic approach to adaptation and transition, are as follows: 1. Promote technological reconversion in exploitation and benefit systems to reduce greenhouse gas emissions in the sector. 2. Promote development of the carbon-neutral initiatives, in order to achieve greater access to international markets. 3. Include, within the energy transition, a Council for Social and Economic Policy–related investment in new technologies for the coal sector, as well as regional adaptation, including the creation of a fund for job-retraining programs. 4. Advance the execution of the Comprehensive Management Plan for Climate Change for the mining and energy sector.
Department government	While La Guajira's economy is heavily dependent on the Cerrejón mine, most of the population relies on subsistence agriculture. The department government also relies heavily on mining royalties from Cerrejón's operations to finance regional and local public investment. The 2020–23 La Guajira development plan is based on five strategic initiatives: 1. A legitimate and strengthened government with improved institutional capacities 2. Moving toward a new diverse and sustainable economy[a] 3. Creating social equity 4. Improving security 5. Developing strategic infrastructure projects for integration of La Guajira[a]

continued

TABLE D.1, *continued*

STAKEHOLDER GROUP	INTERESTS
Cerrejón mine	The Cerrejón mining operation, comprising a large open-pit coal mine plus rail line and seaport, is a joint venture between Anglo American, BHP, and Glencore. It is the largest coal mine in Latin America and one of the largest coal-mining operations in the world, employing more than 6,000 direct employees. Operating since 1985, the mine's current lease runs through 2033. As its starting point, the strategic spatial development planning approach expects that mining companies have a direct interest in supporting broad-based sustainable development in regions where they operate. It also purports that there are many different ways in which companies can look beyond their own operational investments to leverage their activities and their resources in support of socioeconomic and natural-resource-based development.
Civil society and indigenous communities	The communities in which the sector operates are increasingly demanding plans for a future in which they have less dependence on coal. Institutions must be prepared for this forthcoming event. In recent months, a significant controversy between communities and the Cerrejón mine has arisen over concerns that air pollution from mining operations could increase the risk of spreading the COVID-19 pandemic to indigenous communities located in proximity to the mine. This resulted in repeated worker strikes and claims of COVID-19 infection by some workers. Both the Ministry of Mines and Energy and environmental agencies have discarded these claims, based on results from environmental controls and inspection bodies. Beyond disagreements on compliance with environmental standards for air pollution, when it comes to reducing economic dependence on coal mining, there is full alignment of interests between the two stakeholder groups.

Source: World Bank.

a. Note that these entail less than 6 percent of the total budget.